the gift

Mia Dolan was born on the Isle of Sheppey, off the Kent coast, and has been a psychic for nearly twenty years. She works full time as a clairvoyant specializing in psychic predictions and hauntings. Mia is now one of the UK's most trusted and sought-after psychics. She has worked with police and dumbfounded scientific experts. She made intriguing predictions for the press about Princess Diana before her death, and was called to the murder scenes of both Jill Dando and Rachel Nickell. Mia has worked extensively with the media, and has appeared many times on television programmes, including *This Morning*, as well as being the subject of interviews and features in the press. She has also done a great deal of live radio. *The Gift* is her first book. Mia lives in Sheerness and works in Maidstone.

MIA DOLAN

the gift

Element
An Imprint of HarperCollins*Publishers*
77–85 Fulham Palace Road,
Hammersmith, London W6 8JB

The website address is: www.thorsonselement.com

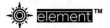

and *Element* are trademarks of
HarperCollins*Publishers* Ltd

First published by Element 2003
This edition published 2004

7

A catalogue record of this book
is available from the British Library

ISBN 0 00 715451 8

Printed and bound in Great Britain by
Clays Ltd, St Ives plc

Author website details:
www.miadolanltd.com

DEDICATION

I dedicate this book to the three absent men
in my life:

my father
my brother
my son

Acknowledgements ☼

I would like to thank:

My daughter Tanya, the most precious thing in my life – thank you for never complaining about having a weird mum;
my mum, for being my place of calm in life's storms;
Jed, for being the best big brother I could have wished for;
Belinda Elliott, for being the sister I always wanted;
Alan Salmon, not only a great friend, but also an inspiration of kindness;
Matthew Parrett, who has been my rock in business and friendship;
Mike Constant, for always being there;
Carol Ashby, who always has her finger on the pulse of life;
Robin Dalton, for her belief in me and her help;
Mark Lucas, for trusting his instinct – and everyone at Lucas Alexander Whitley who put up with my ignorance of the publishing world;
everyone at Thorsons, for their energy and enthusiasm from the beginning;
my nephews, Steven and Arron Dolan, who keep the bond of family strong;
Francesca, Lee and Laura Dolan, thank you for making it great to be an auntie;
Angela and Denise Dolan, having you both as sisters-in-law is a double bonus;
Rosalyn Chissick, without whose authorial skills this book would never have been written.

And, of course, thank you to Eric.

Prologue ☼

'Your toast is burning.'

That is the first thing he ever said to me.

I was in my front room, trying to calm an argument between my children. Tanya was grabbing at Shane's transformer toy and screaming, the TV was blaring – and, in the kitchen, there was bread under the grill.

'Your toast is burning.'

Toast. I had forgotten all about it. I ran back into the kitchen. Flames were licking at the white enamel front of the cooker.

As I wrestled the pan from the grill, I remembered the warning. It was as if there had been a man standing next to me. The voice sounded as if it was outside of me – not inside my head. And yet there was no one in the house, apart from my two children and myself.

I must have been imagining it. That's what I told myself. The mind has a way of making sense of things.

That night as I got ready for bed, I heard the voice again.

'There's nothing to be frightened of, you know.'

Like hell there wasn't. I went into the children's room – they were undisturbed. Tanya's long blonde hair was fanned across the pillow. Her dark eyelashes didn't even flicker. Shane seemed to sense I was there. His blue eyes opened and shut. I crept down the corridor, catching sight of my reflection in a darkened window. I hesitated at the top of the stairs, then combed the house for a radio that might have been left on. Nothing.

A sliver of moonlight made its way between the thick red curtains. Outside – perhaps the voice had come from outside. I opened the front door and looked along the terraced street. It was completely deserted.

'It's perfectly okay, you know.'

'No, it bloody well isn't,' I yelled into the darkness. 'I don't need this and I don't want it. I want it to stop.'

In the early hours of the morning, as I lay beside my husband Andy, our bed began to tremble. A gentle, persistent tremor running along the mattress and through my body. I sat up and looked around the bedroom. The curtains were partially drawn and, through the crack between them, I could see out into the night.

2 a.m. I turned on the lamp and lit a cigarette. I opened my book but I could not read. This had happened before and the tremors were occurring more frequently and with increasing power.

I put my cigarettes and lighter beside me on top of the duvet and picked up my book. The bed trembled again and then slowly, rhythmically, the cigarettes and lighter moved across the bed and onto the floor.

I was going mad.

'Andy,' I tugged at his t-shirt, 'Andy, can you feel it?'

'What?'

'Can you feel the bed trembling?'

And with that it stopped.

'For Christ's sake, Mia.' Andy was tired and grumpy. 'Can I go back to sleep now?'

'Yes,' I said quietly. 'Yes, of course.'

A week later, I went to visit my friend Janet. The door was on the latch as usual and, as I pushed it open, I heard the voice again. A deep, gravelly male voice.

'They're splitting up, you know.'

In the kitchen Janet and I sat at the table, drinking coffee and dissecting our weekends. We'd been friends for years; she had a son and a daughter the same age as mine. Inevitably, the conversation came around to our relationships. I moaned about Andy.

'I had to get up to take the children to school and he's still lazing in bed,' I said.

'Well I've had it,' Janet answered. 'I'm getting out.'

'What do you mean?'

'I'm not putting up with it any longer,' she said. 'I'd rather be on my own.'

Janet told me her plans for leaving Will, but I was not listening. All I could think was that I had known they were splitting up – how had I known it? Janet was not happy in her marriage, but then neither was I. Life was busy and complicated; to get by we put up walls. I knew she was dissatisfied but there were no clues to her leaving, to her and Will splitting up.

I had heard a voice. That meant I was mad. I had lost my reason. What other explanation could there possibly be?

That night the bed did not tremble. But the television changed channels in the middle of a programme, then turned itself off. Going to bed, I switched the light off in the front room and it turned itself back on.

Odd electrical faults occur, I know. But over the next few days, it was as if the lights were enjoying their new-found independence – they dimmed and brightened at will. The television and radio too, had minds of their own, unilaterally deciding when to entertain me.

I bumped into an old school friend, Jennifer, in the high street.

'She's pregnant, you know.'

The voice again.

Nervously, I gabbled at Jennifer, trying to hide my fear. But I had to ask her, I had to know.

'Are you pregnant?'

Jennifer looked at me strangely.

'No,' she said.

'I must be mixing you up with someone else.'

I could not wait to get away. I went straight to my mother's house. She was the only person I had told about the voice.

'I'm going mad,' I said.

'You're tired and in a muddle,' Mum said. 'You're not thinking straight.'

Mum had a logical explanation. My mind was playing tricks on me.

I woke from sleep and I was paralyzed – I could not move any part of my body; I could not even blink. There was a high-pitched noise in my head like a hundred untuned radios. I finally broke out of it and sat upright, feeling as if I had been squeezed into a body that was too small for me.

Jennifer telephoned.

'How did you know?' she asked.

'Know what?'

'I've just been to the doctor and found out I'm pregnant.'

I felt as if I had been punched.

'I told you, I confused you with somebody else,' I said. 'It's just a coincidence.'

'You must be psychic,' Jennifer said.

Psychic? I did not believe in it. Any of it – god or ghosts. Wonderful theories conjured up by humanity's fear of its own mortality. I was an atheist. I believed in what I could touch and see.

A week later, on a Sunday morning, I began hanging up the washing. I lifted a long t-shirt from the laundry basket, started pegging it to the line and, suddenly I was no longer in the garden. Now, underneath my feet, there was not grass, but a stone-strewn slope. And around me were grey rocks and bare, skeletal trees. Where the leaves should have been, there were scraps of torn and bloody clothing. I looked closer. There were limbs in the clothing.

The nose of an aeroplane was 500 feet away from me; the tail section was much further up the mountain. Chunks of twisted metal were scattered everywhere. And bodies. I saw a woman with her head caved in. A burst suitcase. A single child's shoe.

The air was acrid; every time I breathed in, it caught the back of my throat. I could taste it in my mouth. And fear – I was hit by it physically. Two hundred people's fear and pain.

I turned, trying to take it all in and, instantly, I was back in the garden, still pegging Andy's t-shirt to the washing line.

'Oh my god,' I whispered. '*Oh my god*.'

I grabbed Shane and Tanya, who were playing in the garden, and ran straight to my mother's house. All I could think was: 'Get away, I must get away.' As soon as Mum opened the door, I cried, 'It was so real, it was more real than real.'

Mum listened and was calming.

'You went out last night, you're tired and a bit hung over,' she said. 'You probably fell asleep for a moment and had a nightmarish instant. It's nothing to worry about.'

I so wanted to believe her. I went home and cooked dinner, bathed the children, got out the ironing board and began the week's ironing in front of the television. The five o'clock news came on.

'There has been an aeroplane crash in the hills of Madrid,' the newsreader said. 'There are thought to be no survivors. Around two hundred people ...'

The hillside. The burst suitcase. The shoe ...

My heart was pounding but my body was still. When the telephone rang, I went out into the hallway and picked it up.

'Are you watching television?'

'Yes.'

'Are you all right?'

'Yes.'

'We need to talk, Mia,' my mother said.

1

In my earliest memory, I am standing on the doorstep of our house on the Isle of Sheppey, looking out at a group of children playing in the driveway. There is my older brother Jed, my kid brother Peter and our neighbours' children – six of them – all noisily absorbed in games with balls and a scooter. I am watching them and I am thinking: 'I am old enough now to look after you all.' The thought fills me with contentment. I am four years old.

Mum says I was never a child – always a protector. She tells a story of how, at the age of three, I saw an older boy picking on my brother Jed and ran after him with a large stick. I can't remember a time when I didn't want to be taking care of people. It's the way that I am.

I was a quiet child, an observer. Lanky, skinny and very pale, I was always daydreaming. At Sheerness Catholic Primary School, I did not join in much until Peter's first day. It was break time and I was playing on the steps in the playground when I heard a commotion. Looking up, I saw a gang of boys on the grass with Peter trapped in the middle.

I ran over and pushed my way in.

'Leave him alone,' I shouted. 'He's my brother.'

One of the boys turned and looked at me derisively.

'What are you going to do about it?'

I smacked him round the face. Then I kicked one of the other boys in the shins and grabbed hold of Peter's hand. As we walked towards the drinking fountain, one of the 'it' girls – the one with the most sarcastic tongue and the best clothes – said, 'Well done.'

Well done? I don't know whether I hurt the bullies or they were just amazed to see a seven-year-old girl up for a fight, but they left Peter alone. After that, all the coolest people in the school wanted to be around me. I was happy in my skin and that seemed to draw others towards me. I became a ringleader without ever intending to.

I was born into a family that stretched its roots between Italy and Lancashire. My maternal grandmother, Grace Smith, was born and brought up in Malta. Half Italian, she fell in love with Jack Armstrong, an English army officer and, against her mother's advice, married him and came to England. She thought (and he led her to believe) she was en route for a life of luxury. Instead, Jack took her to a mining village in the north of England and life in a two-up two-down, with a lavatory shared with six other houses. It was cold and it rained constantly. She had no use for the ball gowns she had brought with her.

Grace had three children in quick succession – Robert, my mum Kathleen Patricia, and John. She spent most of the war years living in attics in London, working in the ammunitions factory and scrubbing other people's floors. At the end of the war, her husband wrote to say he was not coming home. In barely legible scrawl, he told her he had fallen in love with a female army officer and the two of them were being posted to Germany together.

Grace was furious. The government was keen to reunite families so she wrote to the Home Office, detailing the hardships of a single life with three children and seeking assistance. Her husband was duly threatened with loss of his officer status and, within weeks, tickets arrived for her and the children to join him in Hamburg.

It was a violent sea crossing; everyone was sick. My grandmother was the only passenger on board to sit down to a full cooked breakfast. She was a 4-ft-11 dynamo.

Four years later, Grace, Jack and their three children were posted to army barracks on the Isle of Sheppey. Barren, flat and marshy – the island appeared to Grace to be in the middle of nowhere. The docks and army barracks were busy, but apart from a few small densely populated villages, the island seemed empty. Only a third of it was built on.

My mother, Pat, was 12 years old. A few years later, when Jack started managing the Britannia pub in the biggest of the island's villages, Sheerness, she was often seen in there helping Grace run the restaurant.

It was there my father, Gerry Dolan, first saw her.

Pat was a 20-year-old quarter-Italian beauty with shoulder-length black hair and an hourglass figure. Gerry told his friend, 'That is the girl I am going to marry.'

'Really?' his mate, George, asked impressed. 'Do you know her?'

'No,' my father said, 'not yet.'

At the disco at the Territorial Army Drill Hall later that night, he asked Pat to dance and then walked her home. Gerry Dolan had just come out of the Merchant Navy – he was 31 and had travelled the world. Pat was a shy homebody, but she was quick-witted and known for her wicked sense of humour. They married a year later and, to anyone who ever spent any time with them, it was clearly a marriage of love.

After two years, Jed was born; then I arrived – Marie Elisabeth – and then Peter – all two years apart. We moved around in the very early years – Sheerness, Manchester, back to Sheerness and then St Helens in Lancashire. When I was three years old, we came back to the island and we stayed there – setting up camp at 55 Darlington Drive.

The Isle of Sheppey is eleven miles long and nine miles wide. 35,000 people live there but, during the summer, that figure doubles. There are holiday camps and caravan sites near the water. Apart from tourism, the main trade on the island comes from the docks and the steel mill.

Two thirds of the island is green – and it is flat, very flat. The horizons are enormous. The sunsets fill the sky. King's Ferry is the link to the mainland. Once islanders are on that, they know they're home.

My early years were very happy. My favourite pastime was listening to my parents' record of 'The Blue Danube' and making up dance routines. I was tall for my age and agile. At the age of five, I started to learn ballet at Yvonne West's School of Dance and I became her protégé. 'I had a student before you who went on to be very successful,' she used to say. 'You remind me of her.'

My parents did not really have the money to spare, but they paid for dance classes in church halls several nights a week and scraped together money for the tutus I needed for my exams. Most evenings I took over the front room, pushed the coffee table against the wall, put music on and danced. My parents never coerced me into doing anything – but they did support me, always.

My father, Gerald, was a salesman – a good salesman. Slim and dark-haired, he had incredible charm and gentleness – and he always wore a shirt and tie whenever he left the house. Dad sold everything from central heating and double-glazing to burglar and fire alarms. One year he won the Salesman of the Year award when he sold more books than anybody else at Caxton Books. The prizes on offer were a new washing machine or a holiday in the Bahamas.

Dad said to Mum, 'You choose.'

Mum was still a beauty, with her wavy brown hair and flowery dresses, but she was always, always busy. She looked round the kitchen at the nappies soaking in buckets and said, 'I want the washing machine.'

Dad's income was sporadic. Many evenings Mum ran out of shillings to put in the electric meter and resorted to inserting curtain rings. Many evenings we ran out of those too and so we lit candles and played alphabet games waiting for Dad to come home.

'Animals beginning with A ...'

'Ant, armadillo ...'

'B.'

'Bear, beaver ...'

We would go through the whole alphabet with animals, then move on to countries and films, making a joke of it until Dad came in with the deposit for his next job. Then the lights went back on, Dad opened bottles of beer and Mum went down the road for a Chinese take-away before bed.

The Leas beach was nearby – and it was free – so Mum took us there a lot. We were all at home in the water. We spent wonderful lazy days swimming and looking for treasures along the pebbly waterfront. Often we went with our neighbours – the Stents and the Smiths – so there would be 10 kids making up games. Meanwhile, our mums sat on deckchairs in straw hats, surrounded by carrier bags and bottles of warm squash (which always seemed to get sandy very quickly).

When we wanted an ice cream because all the other kids had one, Mum never said, 'No.' Instead, she would explain why we couldn't have one that day, but as soon as Dad was paid ... We were the poorest family in the street but our house was always full. Everyone wanted to be in our house because it was happy there.

At the weekends, our neighbours would gather around the gnarled apple tree in our back garden and watched the shows we put on. Peter's forte was to hang upside down in the tree – or, hiding his shyness behind the tree, sing his heart out (he had the voice of an angel). Jed, 5-ft-7 at the age of nine, was always the strongman, lifting heavy objects. And I made up ballet dances or, when Jed laid a piece of hardboard on the grass, tap danced a routine.

Dad's dad – Poppa – worked at Warner's Holiday Camp and he used to get us free passes to use the facilities. These included the boating lake and swimming pool – as well as free entrance to the weekly children's feast: chicken drumsticks, sandwiches with lots of butter, and trifles in plastic cases. Every Friday afternoon, we used to come home with party hats, blowers and streamers.

Best of all, I liked to stay at my grandmother Grace's house. She was tiny and dainty and always looked immaculate; her hair and make-up were flawless. She was a great cook and the house always smelled of baking.

I loved to raid her wardrobe and dress up in her old ball gowns. Lace and crinoline, velvet and damask – her dresses were the stuff of fairy tales. She had boxes full of jewellery too; diamonds and rubies mixed together with plastic beads and bangles. I used to pile it on, smear her scarlet lipstick over my face and clomp around in her high-heeled shoes.

Grace's garden was filled with apple and pear trees with gnomes sitting everywhere. I believed that fairies lived in the trees and I was always out there, looking for them.

Jack left Grace just before Mum got married, so Grace took in a lodger. He was in his fifties and his face was craggy and deeply-etched. He wore mismatched jackets, shirts and trousers. He worked at the steel mill and had brown-tinged fingers and dirt under his nails. Uncle Arthur.

One day when I was playing at her house, Grace went out to the shops.

'Do you want to come with me or stay here?' she asked.

I was elbow-deep in her jewellery box.

'I'll stay here,' I said.

'Keep an eye on her, Arthur,' Grace instructed.

She had been gone a few minutes, when Uncle Arthur said, 'Come over here and give me a kiss.'

I looked up from my game.

'You haven't given me a kiss hello yet,' he said.

I was seven years old. I didn't usually kiss him hello – just a peck on the cheek when I was going, to say goodbye. But I went to him and, as I leaned over to kiss him, he pulled me onto his lap. He smelt of the Old Holborn roll-ups he was always making. I kissed him on the cheek.

'Don't be silly,' he said. 'Give me a proper kiss.'

A proper kiss? As far as I knew, that was the same as what I had just done, but on the mouth. My lips touched his, but then his hands went behind my head and he forced my mouth open with his tongue. His tongue went all around my mouth and down my throat.

His tongue was massive and hard. His lips were bristly, press-ing against my face. He put his hand up my skirt and into my knickers. I pushed myself away from him and got off his lap.

'Are you going to put your princess clothes on and show

your Nan how pretty you are?' he asked.

I looked at him in amazement. He was acting totally normally – as if nothing had happened. I was shocked by what he had done; I didn't like it. My gut instinct told me it wasn't right, but I didn't know why.

When Grace got back, her first question to me was, 'Have you been behaving yourself?'

For one moment, I thought of telling her that Uncle Arthur had given me a funny kiss, but he said, 'She's been fine.'

At the weekends, Uncle Arthur worked in Grace's vegetable garden. One afternoon, she said to me, 'Go and tell Arthur I want a cabbage.'

I went down the end of the garden where Uncle Arthur was busy behind the stakes of runner beans.

'Nan wants a cabbage,' I said.

'Come here,' he said, 'and I'll get you one.'

I went towards him and he picked a cabbage.

'Give me a kiss and cuddle,' he said.

'Give me the cabbage.'

Uncle Arthur grabbed me and stuck his tongue down my throat again. Then he put his hand inside my knickers. When, after a few minutes, he stopped, he said, 'There's the cabbage. Ask your nan if she wants any onions.'

Again, he was acting as if nothing had happened. I was confused. Uncle Arthur used the words 'kiss and cuddle'; I knew that was an okay thing to do – he did kiss me and cuddle me, even if he did funny things as well. The fact that he was so normal afterwards compounded the confusion in my head.

Walking back to the house between the fruit trees, I tried to think it all through. I knew if I said anything about what had happened, it would cause arguments and I did not want to be the cause of any problems. What if he said I was lying? What if they didn't believe me?

The next time I stayed the night at Grace's, Uncle Arthur came into my bedroom.

'I've come to give you a goodnight kiss,' he said.

He had his tongue in my mouth the entire time he fiddled with me so that I could not scream or make a noise, but instead I panicked about choking. He put his finger inside me and ran his hands up and down my stomach and legs, but his tongue upset me more than anything else. His tongue was so big, I could not breathe.

When he had finished, he stood up and put the covers back over me.

'You be a good girl then and go to sleep,' he said.

I lay in the dark, confused and frightened. I was terrified he would come back and do it again. I felt horrible – sore and wrong. I lay awake for hours. When I heard Grace go to bed, I went to find her. I knew he would not come to get me in her room.

'I've had a nightmare,' I told her. 'Can I get into bed with you?'

After that, every time I stayed with Grace I pretended I suffered from nightmares. I told her, 'I only feel safe if I'm in bed with you.'

A few days before Christmas that year, Mum sent me down the road to the shop to buy a loaf of bread. Snow had been falling steadily. What I remember is walking home from the shop, rounding the corner and seeing the whole hill ahead of me coated in white – thick, unbroken white – even my footprints had disappeared. I stood in the centre of the road. There was a big, early evening moon and the scene was very bright. I was filled with wonder. Each step was into fresh, new snow. As I walked through the whiteness, I could hear voices – quiet and beautiful high voices. They were singing 'Silent Night'. It was the most beautiful sound I'd ever heard. Mesmerised, I listened as the harmony of the voices enveloped me and filled me with a gentle peace. The sound was so lovely, I joined in with them, singing as I walked down the street.

I had my arms out and snowflakes fell on my hands and face. We sang the hymn three times. When I was at my front door the voices faded away. I was convinced I had been singing with the angels – not because of the voices or the snow, but because of the wonderful feeling in my chest. The euphoria.

'I've just walked down the road singing "Silent Night" with the angels,' I told Mum as she greeted me.

'That's lovely, Mia,' she answered. 'Did you get the bread?'

Mum never made a big deal of anything but later she told me she liked the fact that her daughter could find the magic in things.

Months would go by during which nothing happened, but then I would find myself on my own with Uncle Arthur and he did it all again. Sometimes he put my hand down his old, grey trousers and held it against him. Afterwards, he always pretended everything was normal.

By the time I was nine, I stopped staying at Grace's and Uncle Arthur never got the chance to be on his own with me again. I kept his secret to protect my parents, never telling anyone till now what Arthur did to me.

Every Saturday, we were given half-a-crown each as pocket money. I always knew how I would spend mine: half on a Fab ice lolly and the rest on an assortment of Black Jacks, Fruit Salads, Flying Saucers and other four-for-a-penny delights. I chose chewy sweets because they lasted longest and I liked the feeling of having a great big bag of them.

Sunday lunchtimes Dad went to the Minster Working Men's Club to meet his old friends from the navy and get drunk. He would come back like two of the dwarfs – Happy and Dopey – and we would fleece him mercilessly.

'Let's have a game of cards, Dad,' Jed would say.

Eagerly, we pulled up chairs to the wooden table in the kitchen. Once we got him playing, his pockets were easy pickings. When he fell asleep, Mum took any pound notes off us and put them back into his pocket, but she let us keep the coins. My brothers and I always divided them evenly between us. Sharing was part of the deal.

One Sunday afternoon, Jed called Peter and I outside. He had a ten shilling note. 'Look,' he said. 'I found it on the floor by Dad's trousers.'

We walked down the road to Cheeseborough's supermarket and spent it all on ice cream, chocolates and sweets, coming out with two carrier bags full of booty. We knew we could not go home with it, so we found a workmen's tent on the side of the road. It was striped red and white and we sat in there and munched our way through the lot.

The next day, I took a ten shilling note from Dad's pocket and took it to school. It did not feel like stealing. In the break that day, I called out, 'Who wants sweets?'

I treated the entire class to bounty from the tuck shop in the school hall. The headmaster telephoned Mum.

'Your daughter just bought sweets for the entire class,' he informed her.

Mum covered for me. 'She's probably taken the money she's been saving in her bedroom,' she responded loyally.

When he put down the telephone, the headmaster came to find me. 'Your mother told me you spent all your savings,' he said.

With that, the implications of what I'd done began to sink in. Jed was unsympathetic. 'You're going to get killed, you are,' he jibed at me on the bus on the way home.

'You did the same thing.'

'I know.' Jed did an excellent supercilious older brother. 'But *I* didn't get caught.'

'What have you done?' Mum asked as soon as I got home. 'Where did you get the money?'

'I took it from Dad's pocket when his trousers were on the end of the bed.'

'You've got a lot of explaining to do to your dad when

13

he comes home,' she said. 'I can't believe you stole off your family – you know you get a share in whatever we have.'

What hurt most was the look on Mum's face. It was the first time in my life I had done something terrible. It was two hours until Dad got home and I waited for him in the front room. Sitting on the couch, I tried to watch the television, but I felt too ashamed. I heard Mum and Dad talking in the kitchen, then he came into the room with a newspaper in his hand.

'Now our Mia,' he said (he always called me 'our Mia' because of his Lancashire roots). 'Your mum's told me what you've done and she's sent me in here to punish you.'

He rolled up the newspaper and tapped me on the arm with it.

'Don't do it again,' he said, marking each word with another tap on my shoulder.

The gentlest man in existence, there was no part of him that wanted to hurt me. But, in fact, the hurt was done – the guilt I felt, the total remorse. I never did it again.

And it was never brought up. My family don't hold grudges.

I dreamed of becoming a classical ballerina. When I was 11, I started training to get into the Royal Academy in London. I knew I had to work hard to gain entrance to the Academy, so I put everything I had into it. When you are doing something you excel at, it is a good feeling. But it was hard work.

When the time came for the pre-audition exam, I was very excited and nervous. I was 13 years old and this was the first thing in my life I really wanted. It was important to succeed.

The audition room was huge with wooden floors and

mirrors on the walls – it was everything I had imagined. I danced set moves on the bar and the floor, then it was time for my own routine. I danced to 'The Blue Danube' as I had at home. I was getting changed afterwards, when I was called back into the examination room.

'You have beautiful foot movements,' one of the judges told me.

I flushed with pride. They liked the way I danced.

'And your hand movements are lovely,' another judge said, 'but you should take into consideration, at this point, you could never get entrance into the Academy. We're sorry, but at 5-ft-8, you are too tall.'

Too tall. I was big for my age but no one had mentioned the height requirement to me. For the last two years, all I had done was work and train – five nights a week, every week. It had been a waste of time. All that dancing was useless to me.

On the train on the way home, I sat with the other girls from Yvonne West's school, all of us with our hair in tight buns covered with fine nets. I knew that I was the best dancer among them – yet they, not me, would go on to be dancers. They would have my dream.

I was consoled by the knowledge that I had not failed; it was not because I couldn't dance. I had done my best – now I could go out and play. Freed from the pressure of exams, I discovered boys – or boys discovered me.

My older brother, Jed, looked like Sylvester Stallone and all the girls fancied him. He was a rogue with cropped hair, bleached jeans, boots and braces. He looked every inch the skinhead, but he did not do much fighting. He was too laid-back for that. We hung out together.

The highlight of our week was the under-16s disco in the hall at the Minster Working Men's Club. Dad would spend the evening in the bar, while we – and 50 or so other kids – danced to Diana Ross and The Jackson Five.

One night, I took the short cut through Minster Abbey to the chip shop. On my way to the disco, munching chips and crackling, I saw a nun standing by the wishing well gate. She wore a long blue-black habit and was looking down the hill towards the river. She looked as if she was waiting for somebody. I thought she was in fancy dress.

I was walking towards her, gazing at her, when suddenly she disappeared. I had seen her as clearly as the well gate and the trees and the grass. Now she was gone. I whirled on the spot looking for her, but she had completely vanished. I dumped the rest of my chips in the bin and ran back to the club to find Dad.

'Dad, Dad,' I gabbled, 'I've just seen a nun and she disappeared in front of my eyes.'

His navy chums started laughing. 'You sure you haven't been giving Mia gin,' one of them quipped.

'I'm serious,' I said. 'I saw a nun.'

'Yes Mia,' Dad said with little interest. 'Now go back into the disco.'

I gave up on my friends too. They laughed and I got stroppy. But when I got home, I told Mum what I had seen and she listened.

'Were you scared?' she asked me.

'No – shocked,' I said. 'But not scared.'

'Well that's all right then Mia,' she said.

2

When I was 13, I talked Mum into buying me a pair of blue platform shoes with a two-inch heel. I wore them to the under-16s disco and I knew I looked good. Sheppey Comprehensive was the only secondary school on the island so everyone knew each other: at the disco we mixed with the same people we saw at school. But that night, five new lads turned up. At 17, they were older than the usual crowd. They looked cool, lounging against the wall at the back of the hall.

At 10.30 p.m. the slow dances began and I danced with a couple of gawky 15-year-olds. Then I saw one of the new lads break away from his group. He came towards me.

'Do you want to dance?' he asked.

Tony's hair just touched his shoulders; he had brown eyes and a large, loose mouth. He was wearing a white shirt and it was bright in the disco lights.

'All right,' I said.

I put my hands on his shoulders and he put his hands on my waist. We danced with six inches of space between us. I felt stiff and awkward. It was the first time I had slow danced with someone I did not know – let alone an older guy – and my friends were watching me from the side of the dance floor, giggling.

'Who are you here with?' Tony asked.

I didn't want to say my dad and brother because I thought it would sound uncool.

'My mates,' I said.

'Can I walk you home?'

Walk me home? I knew I looked old for my age and I was chuffed that my friends were seeing me with an older boy, but I was out of my depth.

'No, no,' I told him. 'My mum's picking me up at the end.'

After the dance, Jed came over.

'You all right sis?' he asked me.

'Yes,' I said.

I walked away and left Tony talking with Jed. When the lights came on, I went out to meet Mum in the car park.

'See you,' Tony called out as I walked past.

'Bye,' I said.

When I got home, Jed told me Tony had asked loads of questions about me. He had told him my age – even where we lived. I wasn't interested. It had been a buzz to dance with an older boy, but I did not give him another thought.

Two weeks later, Jed and I went to the County Youth Club two miles away in Sheerness. I was sitting on the couch with my girlfriends when Tony walked in. He was on his own and, after a few minutes, he made a beeline for me.

'Do you want to come out some time?' he asked. 'We could go for a drink.'

'No,' I said, feeling every inch the 13-year-old girl. 'I don't think I'd get into a pub.'

'We'll go to the pictures then.'

I laughed it off. 'No,' I said again. 'I don't think so.'

'You've got a really nice figure,' Tony said. 'Do you know how attractive you are?'

I giggled. I was brought up with brothers so I enjoyed boys' company, but I had never been complimented. I was not used to it. I was not ready for it.

That night, Tony did not leave my side. I could not get rid of him. When the slow music started, he asked me to dance.

'No,' I said. 'I don't think so.'

'Don't be silly,' he said pulling me onto the dance floor.

As we moved, he kept trying to pull me closer and I kept pulling back. As the song came to an end, he started to kiss me. I pushed him away and ran to the toilets; my best friend Michelle followed me.

'That guy fancies you,' she said. 'You going out with him?'

'No,' I said, angrily brushing my hair, 'I'm not.'

To get away from Tony, I slipped out of the youth club and stood in the car park, waiting for Mum.

The next morning, as I hurried late to school, I saw Tony sitting on the wall by the entrance gate.

'I've been waiting for you,' he said. 'Do you want to go out some time?'

'No I don't,' I said. 'I've told you, you're too old and my mum and dad wouldn't like it.'

'It doesn't matter about your parents,' he said, 'would you like it?'

'No,' I said again. 'I have to go, I'm late for school.'

As I walked past him, I heard him shout, 'So when am I going to see you again?'

Uneasy, I called out, 'I don't know' then ran up the long winding path to school.

Two days later, there he was again, waiting at the entrance to the school.

'I thought I'd meet you for lunch,' he said.

I was heading for the chip shop with my friends Michelle and Jane. He started walking with us.

'I'll take you to the pub,' he said. 'We'll have a drink and a chat.'

'I don't want to go to the pub.'

He had his hand on my arm.

'I'm going with my mates,' I said and pulled away.

I sprinted to catch up with my friends but, even inside the chip shop, we could see him waiting for me on the other side of the road. 'He's weird,' Michelle said.

I shuddered. 'I know.'

Two days later, when Peter and I were on our way to the corner shop, Tony jumped out from behind a bush and grabbed my arm.

'Stop running away from me,' he said, 'you know you're my girlfriend.'

'I'm not your girlfriend.'

'Come on,' he said, 'we're going for a walk.'

I pulled my arm away, but he kept trying to grab it. Peter was upset. Gangly and helpless, he was on the verge of tears. 'Leave her alone,' he kept saying. 'Leave her alone.'

Finally, we managed to break away from Tony and ran back to the house. We told Mum what had happened but when she came outside Tony had disappeared.

He was at the school gate again the next morning, wanting to take me to lunch.

'I don't want your bloody lunch, I'm not your bloody girlfriend and I want you to stay away from me, all right?'

I ran into school.

'How can he think I'm his girlfriend when nothing has happened between us?' I asked Michelle. 'Why does he keep on at me when I say I don't want it? I don't understand.'

'The bloke's a loony,' Michelle assured me. 'Stay away from him,' she advised.

That weekend, I was looking out of the kitchen window when I saw Tony's head above the long grass at the bottom of the garden. It was eight o'clock in the morning. He could have been out there all night. Mum picked up a broom and marched outside.

'I'm not doing any harm,' Tony pleaded. 'I just want to talk to Mia.'

'Get out of here,' Mum said. 'Leave my daughter alone.'

'I love your daughter.'

'Well,' Mum told him directly, 'she does not love you.'

Tony had been following me for three weeks and nothing I said made any difference. It was building to a climax. He was scaring me. Mum telephoned the police. They asked if he had hurt me physically and, when she said no, they said there was nothing they could do.

'I'm not going to school on Monday,' I said. 'He'll be there at the gates, I know it.'

'It will all calm down soon,' Mum assured me.

'I'm not going out on my own.'

'The novelty of following you will wear off,' Mum said.

But she agreed to keep me off school for the next few days to cool the situation down.

On Monday, when everyone left for work and school, I went into the sitting room to watch television. Within an hour, I heard a knock at the front door. The glass in the door was patterned and bobbly, but I could see Tony was out there. His face was distorted.

'Go away,' I shouted.

'Why didn't you go to school this morning?'

'Because of you, you weirdo.'

'Let me in,' Tony said. 'We'll talk about it.'

'Go away,' I screamed.

I ran into the front room and shut the door behind me. I sat on a chair and pulled my knees up. I thought if I stayed there he would go away, but his face suddenly appeared at the front room window. He was knocking on the glass.

'Let me in,' he kept saying. 'Come on, let me in.'

'I'm going to call the police,' I said.

I picked up the telephone and dialled Mum's number at work. Tony watched me. Then he went away from the window. Mum came home from work and telephoned the police again, but they still said there was nothing they could do.

For two weeks, I did not leave the house. Three bedrooms, a front room and a kitchen – I wandered between them. I did not want to be left on my own but I knew my parents had to work. Alone in the house, I was terrified. Tony turned up every day.

At first he tried persuasion. 'Don't be silly, let me in,' he said, 'you know we need to talk.'

Then he got angry. 'Open the door, you bitch. You're not fucking me around. I'm going to kill you.'

He used to knock and knock at the windows. I was terrified he was going to break in – at any moment he could get inside the house and hurt me. I telephoned Mum and locked myself in the bathroom. She used up all her holiday time to be with me and Dad came home early from work. All our lives were turned upside down.

Jed was two years younger than Tony, but he was ready to take Tony on. Twice Jed stayed home with me but, on those days, Tony did not come. He knew when I was alone. He was watching the house.

After several calls, the police eventually came to see us. They said that because of the way the law stood, unless Tony physically hurt me or broke into the house, there was nothing they could do.

'We've got to wait for her to be hurt before you do something?' Mum was aghast.

'If we see him in the area, we'll warn him off,' they offered. 'But we cannot arrest him.'

Mum and Dad decided to send me to stay with my grandmother's sister in Devon for a few weeks. I had never met

Great Aunt Mary but all I wanted was to get as far from Tony as I could.

After being stuck indoors terrified for weeks, it was wonderful to be free. I shared a bedroom with my cousin Valerie and learnt to ride horses on the moors. I felt happy again.

I had been in Devon for ten days when, one afternoon, on my way back from the sweet shop, I saw a familiar figure standing under the red brick underpass.

He could not be there – he was hundreds of miles away ...

Tony threw a cigarette to the ground and walked towards me. He looked rough and unkempt; he needed a bath. I was rooted to the spot, too horrified to move.

'I've told your aunt all about you,' he said. 'I've told her you're here because you're a prostitute. She's disgusted with you. She doesn't want to see you. She believes me,' he said. 'She thinks you're dirt.'

I started to cry. Tony changed then; he became suddenly gentle and concerned.

'Don't worry,' he said. 'I'll look after you. I'll get you back to the island.'

I was 13 years old. I was miles from home and I believed my aunt didn't want to see me. He took hold of my arm and we started to walk.

'I shouldn't have said those things to your aunt,' Tony said. 'But I was hurt. I'll make it up to you,' he said, 'I promise.'

Tony walked me to the beach. Along the sea front, there was a Victorian bench seat with a wooden canopy and we sat inside it, looking out at the sea. The bench-hut smelt of urine and was covered in graffiti. There was no one around.

When I eventually stopped crying, Tony said, 'We need to spend some time together, then you'll realize.'

'Realize what?'

'We're meant to be together.'

He was mad. How could he think such a thing?

'If you try to run away I'm going to have to hurt you,' Tony said.

We were inside the wooden hut for hours. I was scared. Really scared. At one point, I saw a man walking his dog by the sea. He was the only person we saw all day – I wanted to cry out to him. But I was terrified.

And I did not know what to say. Tony was being kind to me now, complimentary. He was smiling at me and stroking my hair. How to tell anyone what was going on in this mad world of his? Every atom of my body was screaming to get away.

Tony kept holding my hand and trying to kiss me.

It grew dark.

'It's all right,' he said. 'You won't be scared for long.'

I was numb with shock. After all my efforts to get away from Tony, he was here on his own with me. I was confused and terrified. And I was hungry. All I had to eat were the few squares of chocolate I had bought in the shop just before I saw Tony.

He did not let me leave all night. As daylight dawned, I was desperate to go to the toilet. Eventually Tony agreed to walk me to the public toilets further down the beach.

'Be quick,' he said. 'I'll be waiting outside.'

I went into the ladies' toilets and I heard Tony going into the gents. I had a 500-yard start before Tony saw me – I ran. The town streets were deserted. I thought – hoped – I knew the direction of the police station. Tony was running after me. Closing in on me. I saw lights and charged into the police station at a full run.

'Help, you've got to help me. He won't let me go.'

I was gabbling and crying. Tony burst through the doors.

'She's just upset,' he told the officer calmly. 'A bit hysterical. I'll take her,' he said. 'I'll sort her out.'

Tony was so calm, he sounded plausible. For one awful moment, I thought the police officer was going to tell us both to leave.

'Please don't let him take me,' I said. 'Please phone my parents.'

'Get out of here mate,' the officer said.

They were letting him go, I couldn't believe it.

In the interview room I told my story and, when they learned my age, I had the feeling they realized they should have arrested Tony. They telephoned my parents and put me on a train to Paddington. I scoured the train for Tony then settled into my seat. It was a five-hour journey and I had no money – not even for a cup of tea – but for now, at least, I was safe from Tony.

Dad met me at Paddington Station. He bought me two cans of coke and pie and chips and listened to my story.

'Your aunt telephoned and told us you went to the shops and didn't come back,' he said. 'We were up all night worrying about you.'

'Didn't she see Tony?'

'No,' Dad said. 'He lied to you.'

Dad told me that, while I was away, Tony collared Peter in the street and asked where I was. Peter retorted that Tony would never find me because I'd gone to stay with my aunt in the West Country. A few days later, the house was broken into but nothing was stolen.

'Tony must have broken in and looked through the address book by the phone. That's how he found out where you were,' Dad told me. 'But we can't prove it.'

We were still powerless to do anything to stop Tony invading my life.

I did not see Tony for six weeks. Life began to take on a shape I recognized. I went back to school and started going to the youth club again. Mum and Dad bought me a new summer dress. It was covered in light blue swirls; calf-length with cap sleeves, a v-neck collar and a belt.

I wore it to go to Sheerness. I was meeting my friends at the youth club disco, so I got off the bus at Sheerness bus station and took the short cut through the fairground to the club. I was just walking past the public toilets when Tony appeared in front of me. It was a sunny afternoon but he was wearing a big brown coat.

He had one hand tucked inside the coat and he opened it briefly so I could see he was carrying a knife. The blade was a foot long.

'Come with me,' Tony said.

He closed the coat and grabbed my arm with his free hand.

'If you make any noise at all,' he said, 'I'll stick this knife right through you.'

The fairground was packed – stalls and bumper cars, candy floss, kiss-me-quick hats, music, laughter, noise; so many people. Tony and I walked silently through the middle of it, his knife inches from my skin.

When we reached the sea front, Tony steered us away from the tourist area, towards the docks and up to the grass hill at the end of the beach known as the Greenhill Café. (It was where boys took girls for sex – 'hey darling', that was the invitation – 'want to come up to the Greenhill Café?') It was just that – a green hill – a long way from people and houses. Private. Desolate.

'You think you're so fucking clever,' Tony spat.

He pushed me onto the grass.

'You're a prick tease.'

He was dribbling. I could see flecks of white on his lips. I thought: 'He is going to kill me.' He had mad eyes.

Tony straddled my body. My new dress had buttons all the way down the front and he used the knife to cut them off me, one by one. Then he stroked the knife slowly around my neck, up over my face and down my arms.

'You don't realize how bad you've been,' he said. 'You have caused me a lot of trouble.'

Tony grabbed my arms and held them above my head by the thumbs. The moment he forced himself inside me, I screamed in my head – 'NO'. Then my spirit split away and I was out of my body, floating above. I could see him going up and down on top of me, holding my arms above my head. That day I left my body for the first time.

It did not last long. Tony shuddered and pulled himself out of me.

Then I was back in my body, looking at him kneeling between my legs. He looked smug, satisfied.

'I needed that,' he said.

I did not move or speak.

'Where were you going?' he asked me.

'Home.'

'Come on then,' he said, standing up and tucking himself in. 'I'll get you a taxi.'

Tony had the same air of normality Uncle Arthur used to mask his abuse. The knife was still beside me on the grass. I pulled my knickers up. I felt wet between my legs and very sore.

I held the front of my dress together and we walked back along the beach front. Tony threw the knife into the water. I did not run. There was no point now.

As I got into the back of a taxi, Tony asked, 'How much to take her to Dartington Drive, Minster, mate?' Then he paid the fare.

'See you later,' Tony said, as the taxi drew away.

Sitting in the back of the taxi, holding my dress together, I thought about Mum and Dad. How was I going to tell them what had happened to me? How were they going to feel? I looked down and saw blood on the front of my dress. I looked at my arms. The knife had snagged my skin.

'You all right?' the taxi driver asked me.

'Yes,' I told him. 'I'm all right.'

Damage limitation – that was all I could think about as I walked through the front door. I did not want to hurt my family. I wanted to be strong.

'Mum,' – the words were so big, so final – 'he raped me.'

'Oh God,' Mum was distraught.

She started crying. Then Dad cried, and Peter too. Jed was furious.

'I'm going to rip his bloody head off,' he said.

I just sat there. Very calm, holding my dress around me to keep my body covered. All I felt at that moment was guilt – looking at all the people closest to me, hurting so much.

'I'm all right,' I tried to assure Jed when we were on our own together.

'You've got blood on your dress.'

'Yes, but I'm all right. They'll arrest him now.'

That was the one thought that consoled me. The worst had happened. We had proof now that Tony was dangerous.

I made a statement to the police and they sent a helicopter to look for Tony. We went back to the beach where Tony had thrown the knife, but it had been washed out to sea. Dad drove me to a private clinic for the police medical examination. The old male doctor reminded me of Uncle Arthur. I lay there and let him do what he had to. I did not complain or ask for anything. My first internal exam.

'It's lucky she was a virgin,' the police doctor said. 'There's blood as well as semen. There was proof it was done by force.'

It took hours, but finally I could go home to my family. At last I could take off the dress and knickers he had raped me in. At last I could wash, wash, wash Tony off my skin. The police telephoned to say that they had caught him.

'I'm all right,' I told my family over and over, guilty because they were so upset.

31

Mum ran me a bath. I put on my flannel bear pyjamas and went to bed.

The next day, with all my family around me in the front room, I said, 'He's been locked up. He can't do any more damage now. It's finished.'

And I meant it. I did not want to talk about it. It was over. It's hard to admit this but the stalking was the worst part – worse, even, than being raped. All the time I was confined to the house and Tony kept coming and knocking on the windows, I knew it was leading to something – that it would hit a horrible climax, I just didn't know what that climax would be. Now it had happened. He had raped me. The fear I had been living with for four months was over.

Because of the rape, Tony was locked up and I was safe. I know it sounds crazy but in the relief of the aftermath I was almost glad he raped me. I felt relief – it flooded my body. It could have been worse. He could have killed me.

Tony's friends went to visit him at the remand centre and he convinced them he was innocent. According to him, I had sex with him then made up the story about rape. I wanted the whole thing to disappear, but in a tiny place like Sheppey that was never a possibility.

Tony's friends seemed to be on every street I walked down – and there were a lot of them.

'Slag,' they'd call across the road to me. 'Prick tease.'

I carried on walking, my head filled with just one thought: 'When will this be over? When is it going to end?'

Mum and Dad were immensely kind. They never blamed me – not for one moment. Their love and support was constant and strong. Thinking of ways to make a 13-year-old girl feel better, Dad took out a loan so I could go shopping for clothes. But I was numb, in shock. Everything seemed surreal. I felt dirty, guilty. You see rapes on television and the victims fight. Why didn't I? I had walked through crowds of people with him and I did not scream. I felt ashamed.

The newspapers did not print my name but there is only one secondary school on the island. Everyone knew who I was; everyone was talking about me. Looking at me.

'You're the girl who got raped, aren't you?'

Fearful they would get into fights, I made light of it to my brothers. But I was everyone's curiosity. When it goes to court – I consoled myself – then everyone will know the truth.

I was in the third-year toilets at school one lunchtime when five older girls walked in.

'Everyone but Dolan get out of the toilets,' one of them commanded.

The toilets cleared instantly. These girls were known as bullies. They were fifth years – two years above me – and at 13 that seemed a huge gap.

The biggest of the girls positioned herself by the door. No one else was allowed in or out.

The ringleader – Lorraine – walked towards me and pushed me in the chest.

'You tried chatting up my boyfriend on the bus last night,' she accused.

My mind raced back to the night before. Jed and I had been to the under-16s disco in Leysdown, then caught the bus home. I sat upstairs with Jed and his mates – we were all chatting and laughing, but there was nothing else going on.

'I don't know what you're talking about,' I said. 'I don't even know who your boyfriend is.'

'Everyone knows you're a prick tease,' Lorraine said. 'And a liar. You put a guy inside and now you're after my boyfriend.'

'What do you mean?'

'You're not setting my boyfriend up,' she said. 'You're not getting him into trouble with the police.'

She slapped me round the face.

'Everyone knows what you're like.'

The big girl stayed by the door, but the other four girls started moving in. I was scared. Everything seemed to go in slow motion. I heard a buzzing in my ears. I took two steps back into the toilet cubicle and Lorraine took a couple of steps towards me. I grabbed her by the front of her jumper with one hand, grabbed the cubicle door with the other and smashed it against her face.

She dropped to the floor. I stepped over her back into the main toilet area.

One of the other girls grabbed me by the hair and I turned around and head-butted her. Then it was a free for all. I brought one girl's face down on to my knee and smashed the fourth girl's face on the taps. The big girl by the door ran away.

The buzzing in my ears stopped. I looked around. One girl was hanging over the sink, crying; another was on

34

the floor, moaning. There was blood everywhere. I was horrified.

I could have killed them. The level of my own violence terrified me. I did not know I could fight hard like that. I did not know where the moves came from.

I could still hear the things Lorraine had said. She had me wrong. Everybody had me wrong. I was Tony's victim, not the other way around. This was the first bit of emotion I had shown since Tony raped me, and it came out as rage – wild, uncontrollable rage.

One girl lost a tooth, another had a broken nose. An ambulance was called and I was sent to the headmaster's office. Within minutes, Jed burst in – in all his skinhead splendour.

'I've just heard my sister's been beaten up,' he said. 'Who did it? I'm not having it.'

'Actually, Jed,' the headmaster informed him, 'it's the reverse. Your sister is here because she assaulted four girls.'

The story spread like wildfire: a third-year girl has beaten up five fifth years.

'How did you learn to fight?' girls asked me in the corridors.

I never spoke about it. I was horrified by my behaviour. Before the fight, friends called me 'Dylan' because of my resemblance to the flop-eared rabbit on the TV programme *The Magic Roundabout*. Nothing ruffled me – I was easy going.

Now I had a reputation as the toughest girl at the comp – but I hated it. At the time of the fight I wanted to stop

Lorraine and her gang – that was all I knew. I felt like a cornered rat and I did not want to be hurt again. My body had been attacked too many times. I had proved I was not defenceless, but I felt terrible about what I had done. I wanted it to go away. I wanted to be left alone.

Three weeks later, I was walking home from school when the fifth-form girls jumped on me again – this time from behind a clump of bushes. They knocked me unconscious. When I came round, Michelle took me to the medical centre.

I did not want to fight but I knew strength was the only thing Lorraine would understand. I got her on the path near the school a couple of days later. 'This can go on forever,' I said. 'I can beat you up now then you can come after me with your mates and then I'll get you again …'

She looked at me; I could see she was nervous.

'What do you want to do?' I asked her.

'Leave it,' she said.

I let her go. I hoped that was an end to it.

But the taunting never stopped. Tony had branded me – on the outside as well as inside my skin. Only my family believed me. My family and my best friend, Michelle. Now we were both outsiders – me because of what Tony had done to me, and Michelle because she was the only mixed race child in the school. We stuck up for each other, always.

One day we were lazing on the grass at school, smoking illicit cigarettes when two fifth-year girls came up to us. 'What year you in?' they asked.

'Third.'

'Give us your dinner money.'

'What?' Michelle was amazed.

'Give us your dinner money.'

'Do you know who she is?' Michelle motioned towards me.

'No,' the girls' tones were sarcastic. 'Who?'

'Mia Dolan.'

There was a moment of silence. 'You can keep your dinner money,' the girls said.

'Yeah, right.'

We kept our money – and took every penny they had on them. Our pockets were bulging. We took it all back to the third-year common room and emptied it onto the table. Keeping the money would have made us as bad as them. There were kids in that room who had had nothing to eat.

The trial took 10 months to come through. I did my best to get on with my life until then. One night Jed and I snuck out of the house to a party at the end of the street. It was a summer evening; 100 teenagers getting drunk on cider and vomiting in the bushes. Around 1 a.m., the record player broke.

We could see Sheerness Comprehensive School at the end of the road.

'There's a tape machine in the art block,' Jed said. 'I'll go to the comp and get it. I'll put it back tomorrow,' – the plan was perfect. 'No one will ever know it was missing.'

Jed got into the art block through the louvre windows and

returned, half an hour later, with a new music system. The party was on again.

Two hours later, we heard police sirens and came out onto the street. The art block was on fire – two floors, half the size of a football pitch. The sky was ablaze. Horrified, everyone looked at Jed. 'What the hell have you done?'

'I haven't done anything.' Jed was amazed.

'Well, how come the school is on fire?'

'Fuck,' Jed said, 'I was smoking a cigarette.'

'Where did you put the cigarette?'

He hesitated, as he thought about it.

'In the bin.'

'What else was in the bin?'

'Paper, I suppose, it is an art block …'

The next day, the police came to our house.

'We have reason to believe your son Gerald went into the art block last night and caused a fire,' the police officer said.

Mum was appalled. No one in our family had ever been in trouble with the police. Besides, she had seen us all go to bed the night before.

'I can vouch for Jed,' she said. 'He was here all night.'

But talk of the fire was all around the island. The stress was too much for Jed. He told Mum the truth.

'I didn't mean to burn the art block down,' he told her. 'What do I do?'

The police came back.

'The louvre windows to the art block were broken,' the police said. 'There was blood on the glass. It is important we find out who did it because the glass was coated with highly poisonous substances.'

Jed had cut his arm on one of the broken louvres.

'It was my son,' Mum said.

The police were lying about the poison, but they had got Jed.

While Jed was awaiting trial, we got a telephone call from the police to say that Tony's case would be heard in the Crown Court in Maidstone in 10 days time.

'Your daughter will need to be there.'

'Will you be all right?' Mum asked me.

I told her I would be fine. I went out into the garden and sat in my favourite spot, by the apple tree. I could not stand the thought that Mum and Dad would be upset again. I did not want to be the cause of their pain. Tony was pleading not guilty. I wondered if the judge would believe me. And if he did, would everyone finally stop singling me out?

In court the first day, a police inspector took us into a side room and told me, 'You will be in the witness box for a few days and it will be harrowing for you, but stick to the truth and you'll get through it.'

My parents were not allowed in with me, as they had to give evidence later. When I went into the courtroom, the police inspector warned them, 'Your daughter is going to be ripped to shreds in there. She'll be an emotional wreck and will need a lot of putting back together.'

As I walked into court, my heart was hammering. I had not seen Tony since the night of the rape. I was scared. As I was shown into the witness box, I glanced over to the dock where Tony was sitting. He was wearing a white shirt and a black tie. He smiled at me. A smile that seemed to say: 'You have no chance.' A smile that said he was still in total control.

I was 14 years old. I knew everyone expected me to turn into a wreck, but Tony's smile was the final incentive I needed. There was no way I was going to fall apart.

Over the next few days, Tony's barrister went to town on me.

'The dress you were wearing was very close fitting,' he said. 'Did you feel sexy in it?'

'No.'

'Isn't it the sort of dress you buy to feel attractive?'

'No. It was a present from my mum and dad.'

'I put it to you, you enjoyed and were flattered by the attentions of this young man. You had arranged to meet him that day when you said you were going to the youth club. You panicked after having sex with him because of what your parents would say ...'

And on and on ...

'I put it to you that the nicks and scratches on your arms were a result of you getting carried away by passion ...'

'No.'

'Then why didn't you scream or run? Why didn't you tell the taxi driver what had happened to you? Why weren't you upset during your interviews with the police after the event?'

I did not get upset or angry. I answered the questions slowly and carefully. At the end of the first day, I came out of the courtroom and Mum asked if I was all right.

'Yes,' I said, deliberately upbeat. 'Are we going home now? I'm starving.'

The inspector came up to us as we were leaving. He smiled warmly at me and said, 'Regardless of age, I have never seen a woman keep it together as Mia did in the witness box today.'

I was in the box for two days; then my parents went in. The trial lasted three weeks but, for the rest of the time, we stayed away. When the telephone call came, it was a huge relief.

'Tony Brown has been found guilty,' the police officer told us. 'He has been sentenced to seven years in prison.'

3

It was a hard time for my family. Jed's court case took place just two months after Tony's. We were quietly confident that, having never been in trouble with the law before, he would be given a suspended sentence. We were trying to put tragedy behind us; we wanted to be united. Together in strength.

Jed's case lasted a day. When the judge sentenced him, he said, 'We accept it was not arson, but the fact remains that if you had not been in the art block, it would not have burnt down.'

Jed was sentenced to 'six-two' – anything from six months to two years in Borstal. We were all shocked – it was an accident. Jed was not malicious, it was the first thing he had done wrong.

Two weeks later, Dad slipped a disc. He ended up in hospital and could not go back to work for three months. He had no insurance and we got behind with our mortgage and car repayments. We took out an overdraft.

'I'll be back at work next month,' Dad said cheerily. 'We'll soon sort this lot out.'

He had been back at work for two weeks when he contracted double pneumonia and was back in hospital. He was very ill. This time he was off work for four months.

'If you don't stop drinking and smoking,' the doctor told him, 'you will be dead within two years.'

Dad stopped his excesses for a couple of months – he was scared by the doctor, as we all were. But it did not last.

'I'd rather have a short and happy life than a long and miserable one,' Dad said, reaching for his Player's Navy Cut. It was always the way he lived. At the age of 18 he joined the navy and, by the time he met Mum, had more tales to tell than anyone I knew. He lived hard.

The tale of Dad's encounter with a shark was my favourite: 'I was painting a ship in deep water and a shark swam beside me,' he would say. 'So I leant over and painted my initials on him. Somewhere out there' – his tone was wistful – 'there is a shark swimming around with my name on his back.'

'It's not true,' I'd say, fervently hoping that it was.

'It is true, our Mia,' he always maintained.

Now, weak and ill, Dad was declared bankrupt. We lost the house and car. Mum had started working as a secretary at the steel mill and she managed to talk them into giving us a flat they owned inside the docks. So we moved to Regency Close, an old naval terrace block.

The flat was posh but only had two bedrooms, so my brothers and I set up camp in one room. We did not mind – we were so relieved the oppression of debt was behind us. It felt like a fresh start.

Jed kept his nose down in borstal and was released after seven months. But he came back to us changed. He was skin and bone, covered in sores and scars. At home, we still found the soft old Jed, but on the streets, he was mean. He could take on anyone. Before, when people called him names, he laughed it off, it did not matter. Now he was much more likely to head butt them instantly.

I had hoped Tony's court case would vindicate me, that it would make everybody accept the truth. But although Tony went to prison, he never admitted his guilt, so the same people who blamed me for his arrest now blamed me for the fact he was locked away.

No boys would ever ask me out. I knew I looked okay (when I went off the island, lots of boys wanted to be around me) – it wasn't the way I looked, it was the stigma I carried. Local boys still worried I'd set them up and go to the police with false accusations. I missed out on a lot of ordinary teenage experiences.

Walking into the church youth club, a skinhead grabbed hold of me. 'Oi, Dolan,' he leered. He tried to put his hand down the front of my dress and I pushed him off.

'Come on,' he said, 'you know you like it.'

I thought: 'He is doing this because it's me – Mia Dolan – he wouldn't do this to anyone else. He thinks I'm dirt.'

I headbutted him and, as his head fell forwards, I brought my knee up into his face. He was down in two moves. There was blood everywhere. I walked past him into the youth club.

'Well done,' Michelle said.

I did not feel that way. As with the girls in the toilets, all I knew was that I had to stop him. I couldn't let him – or anyone – do that to me again.

Crispin was my first boyfriend. He lived at Warden Point on the cliff tops in an old coastguard cottage with his dad. His younger brother Lucien was in my class at school. I spent six weeks in Wales with him, staying with his mum. It was tremendously hot.

Crispin was incredibly gentle. We used to go for walks and he would hold my hand and we would kiss. Crispin knew the names of all the birds and I watched him whisper to wild horses. Crispin enthralled me. He was not like any of the boys I knew. Our relationship fizzled out after a few months, but he was one of the few boys to treat me fairly. And he did not try to have sex with me. He was perfect.

I spent the summer of my fifteenth year at the sea. There was a big wooden box with an anchor, 200 yards off the beach which we called The Float. Often there would be 30 or more teenagers, sitting on it, diving off it or rocking it backwards and forwards.

I had a golden tan and a wicked figure. But I still had no interest in sex. I hung out with my brothers and their mates and loved their company, but boyfriends were grief I didn't need. I was convinced the rape had put me off sex. Until I met Gareth.

Gareth worked behind the bar in The Royal pub where we

all used to congregate after the beach. He was 18 years old and 6-ft tall, with thick white-blond hair and tanned skin. He wore cap-sleeved t-shirts and love beads around his neck. All the girls fancied him.

I walked in one afternoon in my cut-off denim shorts and bikini top and he called me over.

'Do you fancy coming back later?' he asked. 'I've got some time off. We could sit and have a chat.'

'Okay,' I said, 'if you want.'

I went back at seven and we sat at the bar. Gareth was from Wales and that intrigued me. I went back to see him the next day, and the next. We kissed, but whenever he tried to take it further, I laughed it off and pulled away. He was very sweet about it. He never pressurized me or took offence.

We had been seeing each other for six weeks when we went to a friend's sixteenth birthday party. There was lots of cider and beer and, for the first time in my life, I got really drunk.

'You better come back to my place and sober up before you go home,' Gareth suggested.

We staggered back to his room in the guest house above the pub. We had sex but I was in such a drunken haze I don't remember whether I enjoyed it or not. I came round at 2 a.m. Gareth was lying naked beside me. I realized what had happened and ran home.

When I saw Gareth the next day, we did not mention it. Instead, we carried on where we had left off – kissing and talking.

My period was late. I made an appointment to see the doctor without telling anyone. When he told me I was pregnant, I could not believe it. I'd had sex once in a drunken haze.

I left the doctor's surgery and walked straight to the hotel where Gareth worked. It was too early to find him in the bar, so I went to his room. The door was open and I walked straight in. He was in bed with my friend Jane.

They saw me at the same moment and pulled apart.

'You bastard,' I said. 'I've come here to tell you I'm pregnant and you're in bed with my mate.'

'You don't know it's mine,' Gareth said instantly.

I could not speak. I walked out. In my head I started a conversation with him: 'You're the only person I've slept with, I thought I could trust you ...'

Then I went straight to a pay phone and called Mum.

'Can you meet me at lunch time?'

'Is anything the matter?'

'No,' I lied. 'I just want to talk to you about something.'

I sat on the beach. It felt so unfair. All my mates were having sex all the time and the one time I had, I fell pregnant. Mum was going to freak. I thought of the pain the rape had caused her. There was no way I could keep a child. It was not an option. Besides, I did not see it as a baby – it was just a mess. A nightmare I had put on the family again.

I wanted this all to be over as quickly and cleanly as possible, but I was still only 15 and legally I needed Mum to sign the papers. Mum is Catholic; she does not believe in abortion. It would kill her to have to go against her faith.

I met Mum in the café at the railway station. I got us a cup of tea each and then sat opposite her at the laminated table.

'Listen Mum,' I said with all the determination I could muster. 'I'm pregnant and I'm going to have an abortion.'

Mum started crying. Her pain cut into me, but I could not stop now.

'If you don't sign the consent papers,' I continued, 'then I'm going to put myself into voluntary care and get it done anyway.'

'You don't know what you're doing,' Mum said.

'I absolutely know what I'm doing,' I told her. 'It's not your decision. It's mine. You do not have a choice.'

I looked at her, sad and broken in front of me.

'I don't want to talk about it,' I said.

Every inch of me wanted to hug Mum and have her hug me. But I had to see this through. I had to be strong for us both. I stood up.

'I'll phone the doctor this afternoon and make an appointment for an abortion as soon as possible,' I said.

I left Mum in the café. My heart ached, but I did not cry.

In the days that followed, I kept my own counsel. I could cope with this – I knew I could. I did not need to burden anybody. I had already put my family through enough.

On the day of the abortion, I let Mum drop me off at the hospital and sign the papers, but I did not want her to stay. I was self-contained, totally in control. I could see Mum was hurting, but I couldn't afford to let her question what I was doing.

The nurses treated me like dirt. They made me feel like the little whore they assumed I was. I bit my tongue, wanting to yell at them: 'It was my first time, how do you think this feels for me?' but I held it all inside.

I had horrific nightmares. I would be running through corridors in a big building, looking for the baby I could hear crying. Running, opening doors, running, looking to find the baby. I never found it, although I looked for it every night for seven months.

I used to wake in the room I shared with my brothers, sweating, tears rolling down my face. I would creep along the hall to the bathroom and wash my face. I never told anyone I had nightmares. If you love someone, you don't visit your pain on them. And I did not want kindness. There was a raw place deep inside me which I wanted to protect at all costs.

4

Sheerness was a busy dock. The bars were filled with seamen from all over the world. Local lads would spend the night, trying to talk them into free drinks. Money was always scarce and the seamen were on holiday.

One night, sitting in the Britannia pub with Michelle, I saw Jed and Peter in conversation with two seamen – they kept looking across the makeshift dance floor at us.

'All right sis?' Peter said, coming up to me and putting his hand on my shoulder. Peter was 14, but looked years older. I could see in his eyes that he was up to no good.

'What do you want?' I asked him. 'I haven't got any money.'

'I don't want anything,' Peter said, smiling over at the seamen. 'I'm just making sure you're okay.'

A few moments later, Peter returned. 'Don't lose your temper Mia,' he said, 'but you've got to go home now. Go through the toilets in the other bar and sneak out.'

'Like hell I will.'

'You don't understand,' Peter tried again. 'We've just sold you.'

Michelle burst out laughing.

'What do you mean you've bloody sold me?'

'Ssssssh.'

Peter was standing in front of me, obscuring my view of the men at the bar.

'We got £30,' Pete said. 'We'll give half of it to you.'

'I don't want it.'

'We've already drunk some of the money,' Pete said. 'You've got to go. If you don't there'll be a hell of a row.'

Michelle was still laughing. 'I'll go with you,' she volunteered.

I knew if I did not leave, there would be a fight. I had no choice. As I walked past the bar to escape out of the toilets, one of the seamen raised his glass at me and smiled.

To add insult to injury, Jed and Pete blew the money before they got home – I never saw a penny of it. I could not go into town for days, waiting for the Dutch ship to sail. Worse still, a few months later they did the same thing again.

I should have been outraged but I knew it was a prank. They would never have let the slightest harm come to me. They felt guilty for selling me and spoilt me a lot.

21 January, 1977. I was in the flat on my own, when a friend of Jed's, Mick, turned up. We decided to walk into town together. As we stepped out into the hall, we heard a scream. We ran to the balcony and saw a boy falling down the spiral staircase.

'Oh my God.'

We both started running down the stairs. We could hear the boy crashing and banging his head against the walls, tumbling and screaming. He hit the concrete at the bottom – then he disappeared.

I had not taken my eyes off him for a moment yet he had vanished. There, in his place, were shafts of light with dust particles floating through them.

'What happened?' Mick asked. 'Where's he gone?'

I had a huge lump in my throat; I wanted to cry.

'I don't know,' I managed to say.

Mick ran down the stairs to the basement. I went out the front of the flats and looked all around. We were convinced the boy was somewhere there.

'This is really weird,' Mick said.

When we were totally sure that the little boy was nowhere around, we started walking towards the town.

'You did see a little kid fall down the stairs, didn't you?' Mick asked again.

'Yes – he fell from the first floor, I think.'

'And landed at the bottom of the stairs, by the front door.'

'He was wearing dark knee-length shorts and boots,' I said.

'Yes,' Mick agreed. 'Old-fashioned posh clothes.'

We checked and rechecked the details of what we had seen.

'It must be a ghost,' Mick said at last.

It was his idea to try to see if we could find out anything about the boy. We went to the library and asked to look through their old newspapers. We sat with the front pages of every local weekly newspaper for 50 years and began our search. All we knew was that we were looking for a story about a little boy in Blue Town where I lived. It took hours, but by late afternoon we had it.

'I've found it, I've found it,' Mick was exultant.

We pored over the story of a tragic accident: a boy had fallen down stairs, fractured his skull and died. 'And look at the date,' Mick said.

I peered at the top of the paper. 21 January, 1927.

'Fifty years ago, to the day.'

We were very quiet after that. Shocked. All the time we had been looking, I realized, I had not expected to find anything. On the walk to the pub to meet Jed and his mates, Mick did most of the talking. My head was full of so many thoughts: ghosts actually existed; that was the first thing I had to take on board. I remembered the nun I had seen in the Abbey churchyard; she had mysteriously vanished in front of my eyes. If ghosts *did* exist, then that opened a gateway to so much more.

It was still daylight when we got to the pub on Sheerness High Street. Mick started regaling everybody with our story, but I did not want to speak about it, not then. I left the pub and went home. Walking back into the flats, I passed the place where the boy had fallen. I did not feel nervous, in fact, throughout, I had felt strangely calm.

'How did you feel walking back up the stairs?' Mum asked later.

'All right.'

'That's fine then,' she said. 'It will probably be another fifty years before anyone sees the boy again.'

The sense of mystery brought Mick and I together. We were always talking about the ghost. I spent most of my time with my brothers and their mates, so it was natural for Mick and I to hang out together.

Mick was 6-ft-2 with light brown hair and very, very blue eyes. He had tattoos on his lower arms and he was cool – he could fight, had a car and always had money. Gradually, we moved from being friends to being boyfriend and girlfriend. I liked him because he was funny and sweet and wasn't always trying to have sex with me. Mum was not happy. Mick was a rogue with a criminal record and he was six years older than me.

'I don't want you to see Mick,' she said.

On my sixteenth birthday, friends threw me a surprise party at one of their houses. That night, Mick said, 'I can't get a job here – I'm going back to Ipswich. Why don't you come with me?'

'Go to Ipswich?' It was an outrageous suggestion. 'I can't just go.'

'You can do anything,' Mick said. 'You're sixteen now.'

The next morning, Mum and I were in the kitchen.

'Did you have a good birthday?' she asked me. 'What did you do?'

'Michelle threw me a party,' I said. 'I went with Mick.'

'I thought I asked you not to see him.'

'You can't tell me what to do,' I told her. 'I'm sixteen.'

'I'm telling you not to see him again,' Mum said.

I had never seen her like this. Then she uttered the fatal words that changed our lives. 'All the time you are under my roof,' she said, 'you will do as I say.'

We had the biggest argument we have ever had. When she went out, I packed a bag and went to the house where Mick was staying.

'What's with the bag?' he asked when he saw me on the step.

'I've decided to come to Ipswich.'

It was as simple as that. We climbed into his battered old Mini and left for Ipswich the same day. I had no idea what I was doing. I was playing at life. Goodbye school, goodbye friends, goodbye Jed, Peter, Mum and Dad. It was a spur of the moment decision. I was on an adventure.

That first night in Ipswich, we stayed at Mick's friends' flat. They pulled out a couch in the lounge for us and the girl brought in a bundle of blankets. They took it for granted Mick and I were sleeping together, but we had not had sex yet. I felt awkward and a bit afraid.

I was used to having to be home at a certain time – and it hit me suddenly: I didn't have to be anywhere, I had left home.

Mick was very gentle. It was the first time in my life I had had sex willingly. I felt safe with Mick, but the best bit was the cuddle afterwards – his arms around me as I went to sleep.

Very quickly, we got a tiny one-bedroom flat in the centre of Ipswich. Mick got a job welding and I started working in a sausage factory. Standing at a conveyor belt for seven hours a day, patting sausages into sausage shapes. On the second day, I lasted half an hour, before ripping off my regulation hairnet and marching to the manager's office.

'There must be something more interesting I can do than press sausages together,' I told him.

'Well,' he said, 'if you think you can handle it, I'll put you in meat-cutting.'

He showed me to a massive warehouse where 18 men were cutting carcasses to pieces with electric knives. I stayed 20 minutes, then resigned.

After a few days, I telephoned Mum.

'Come home dear,' she said. 'Come home.'

'I'm not coming home Mum,' I said. 'But I'm all right, honest. I'll come and see you soon.'

'Just come home.'

I kept the phone call short, refusing to give her my address. I felt guilty. I told myself she would get used to it, in time.

My next job was in a vegetable factory: peeling onions by the hundred. I got paid per sack. Every day, for the first hour, my eyes streamed so much I could not see. Then I toughened up. Going home on the bus, people would move away from me. The smell was unbearable.

Two months later, I landed a job in a joke shop. I spent my days surrounded by itching powder, soap that went black, plastic poo, fake cigarettes and cigarettes that were really fireworks. Kids used to come in and throw a stink bomb back into the shop as they fled.

When I was not at work, I played house. I was shopping and cooking for the first time. The thrill of buying my first biscuit tin. I picked daffodils from the park and put them in a milk bottle on the mantelpiece. I bought a packet of 20 cigarettes for the first time: a whole packet of 20 for myself.

A new Pizza parlour opened in town and I got a job there, waitressing in the evenings. The staff were mainly Italian and made the pizzas, fresh, in front of the customers. I enjoyed my job, earning a lot in tips. At first, Mick used to meet me from work when I finished, then he started going out with his mates instead.

'You're at work,' he grumbled. 'What do you expect me to do?'

He got home later and later. One night I sat up until two in the morning, waiting for him, anxious that something awful had happened.

Jed and Theresa, his girlfriend, came to visit and we all decided to move into a house together in Cobbold Street. The house was old and dirty but we bought a giant pot of cream paint and painted the whole place. We got a skinny whippet-cross off the street; we called it Nipper.

We had been in Ipswich for three months, when Mick and I had our first big row. I had bought dinner and a bottle of wine. He wanted to go out with his mates.

'You can't go out,' I told him. 'We are meant to be having an evening in.'

He put his coat on. 'I'm going out.'

I grabbed his coat. 'No you're not.'

He slapped me round the face and walked out of the door.

I opened the bottle of wine and drank my way through it. When Theresa got back later that evening, I locked myself in the outside toilet. I did not want to talk to anybody, I wanted to be left alone. But, looking around the kitchen, Theresa spotted an empty bottle of sleeping tablets and convinced herself I had taken an overdose. She telephoned the police and an ambulance.

I came round in the hospital as they were putting a tube down my throat.

'What are you doing?'

'You've got to have your stomach pumped.'

'I haven't taken anything.'

But Theresa's hysteria was more convincing than my drunken insistence.

'We know you have and if you don't do this nicely, we'll have to section you. Your life is at risk.'

I was sent home, hung over and with a sore stomach and throat. Mick was in the front room, in semi-darkness. I thought he was going to apologize; I was ready to kiss and make up, but instead he went into the kitchen and got the bread knife. He offered me the handle.

'If you're going to kill yourself,' he said, 'don't fuck around – do it properly.'

Jed and Theresa left after a month. They missed the island. I missed them but this was my life now. And Mick was being kind again – although he never apologized.

One evening, a girlfriend of one of Mick's mates came into the pizza parlour to see me.

'I think you ought to know,' she told me, 'while you're at work, Mick is seeing another girl.'

We had been living together for six months. I thought we

were in love. Everything on which I was building my life was crumbling. I felt the room spinning. I needed to see Mick. I asked my boss for the evening off, went home and waited there.

Mick came home in the early hours of the morning. He had a love bite on his neck.

'I know you're seeing another girl,' I told him.

'You're right,' he said. 'I am. And I just found out she's got gonorrhoea so you better get yourself to the clap clinic.'

No remorse. No asking for forgiveness – or promising not to do it again. Mick knew I was hurting and he did not care. I had left home and worked at dead-end jobs because I put my trust in him. And it had been a lie. He was not the man I thought he was.

That night I slept in Jed and Theresa's old bedroom. The next day, I went to the hospital on my own. I was 17 years old, embarrassed to even ask where the venereal disease clinic was.

'The clap clinic,' I whispered to a foreign nurse in the corridor.

'Clap?' She had no idea what I was talking about.

I squirmed with embarrassment. 'The dose.'

'The dose?'

'I think I might have gonorrhoea.'

'Oh, the STD clinic,' she said in a loud and cheerful voice. 'It's round the back of the hospital.'

I was examined and various tests were carried out, then I was shown into the doctor's office.

'You haven't got gonorrhoea or any other sexual transmitted

disease,' the doctor told me. 'But did you know you're pregnant?'

I'd come to check whether I had the clap because I had a boyfriend who didn't give a damn about me, and now I was being told I was having his child.

'You're two months pregnant,' the doctor said.

I sat in shocked silence.

'Do you want a termination?'

'I don't know,' I said. 'I need to think about it.'

I sat in the park by the lake. There were swans on the water and overhanging willow trees. I thought about the abortion I had two years earlier. The vivid nightmares.

I couldn't have another abortion – that was the only thing I knew for certain. So what the hell was I going to do? I would not stay with Mick – the relationship would not last, I knew that. Where would I live with a baby? Should I tell Mum and Dad? Having a baby was an enormous thing to do.

I went home, prepared dinner and waited for Mick.

'Did you go to the clap clinic?' he asked me.

'Yes.'

'And?'

'I haven't got anything,' I said, 'but I am pregnant.'

Mick was quiet for a moment, then his reaction stunned me.

'That's brilliant,' he said.

I tried to match his excitement, but it was not in me. He had hurt me too deeply. I was already pulling away.

Mick and I stayed living together as a couple in the house we rented on Cobbold Street. I was five months pregnant and still my parents did not know. Mick's mum, Lillian, was kind to me: a mother substitute. Gentle and generous, she was always turning up with bits for the new baby, which I thanked her for and then hid away in the back room. Babygros, little cardigans, cot blankets – even a Silver Cross pram.

I went to the doctor's for the first time and was given a prescription for iron tablets and information about antenatal classes.

'You need to see a midwife,' he told me.

I ignored his advice and threw away the prescription. I didn't know what to do about the fact I was pregnant, so I refused to think about it. My stomach was growing, but I did not view it as anything other than a bump.

Mick was out all the time now. Sometimes Lil took me to bingo, as my own mum would have done. She made me feel a little less lonely.

I went to see my parents for the first time since I left home. I was seven months pregnant, but I was wearing a loose dress. I hoped Mum wouldn't notice. We sat in the garden and she looked at me.

'You're pregnant.'

'So?' I was immediately defensive.

Flustered, words tumbled out of her mouth. 'What are you going to do? Are you ready for a baby? Are you nervous about giving birth? Have you got all the stuff you need? Are you happy?'

'It's sorted Mum,' I told her. 'Let's not talk about it.'

She had told me not to go with Mick, but I had been bloody-minded. I'd made a huge mistake. Mum would never have said, 'I told you so,' but I was still too stubborn, too proud to say, 'Mick is screwing around and I am living a hand-to-mouth existence on the dole.'

I sat with her in the garden – everything was so familiar, exactly as I remembered it. I thought: 'I'm going to have a baby – for me it can never be the same.' I thought: 'My child-hood is finished.' My small space of freedom was over.

I had been considering staying at home with Mum and Dad and Jed and Peter. I thought maybe I could start again. But now I was with them, so different from the person I had been, I was ashamed of the mess I was in. I could not inflict myself on them. I could not stay. *I* had made a life for myself and *I* had to sort it out. I stood up and walked to the door.

Mum was crying. She did not want me to go. I cuddled her on the doorstep. Dad was upset too.

'You don't have to go back,' he said, 'you can stay here.'

'I can't stay here,' I said. I tried to keep my tone upbeat. 'I've got a nice place in Ipswich, Mick's mum's really lovely and my relationship is fine. As soon as the baby is born, I'll be down to show it to you,' I promised.

On the train taking me back to Ipswich, rain hit the window and I felt more bereft than I ever had. When I left home, I was laid-back and unrufflable; nine months later I was pregnant, vulnerable, broke and in a bad relationship. I had made every mistake I vowed I never would. I wanted to be at home, but the life I knew wasn't there anymore. I had lost my last hope – the hope that I could go home.

What have I done? I asked myself.

I was 17, but old for my age; battle scarred, but optimistic. I thought once I had the baby, everything with Mick might work out. The baby would bring us together. I hoped once I got my figure back he would stop playing around.

We spent Christmas day with Mick's parents and I ate and ate to push everything else away. In the afternoon, Mick went out to see his mates. He never came back. I sat in the lounge with his parents and my bump. I grew increasingly uncomfortable and embarrassed. How could he do this to me?

The baby was not due for three weeks, but as I went to telephone for a taxi to take me home, I doubled over in pain. Lil felt my stomach – it was hard as a football, but because I refused to know anything about my pregnancy, I had no idea this was a sign the baby was coming. Lil called an ambulance.

'As soon as Mick turns up, I'll tell him you're at the hospital,' she said.

The rest of that night felt like a punishment. The hours went by; Mick never came. I was in heavy labour, but the nurse refused to believe me. I asked for painkillers, but she insisted I had hours to go.

The pain was excruciating. I had never read a book about babies, never attended an antenatal class, never spoken to my mum or any other woman about what I might expect. I hung over the back of the bed, then I got on my hands and knees and crawled around. I was in so much pain, I did not know what to do with myself.

I rang the buzzer, 'I think the baby's coming.'

'You've got hours to go yet.'

'Please,' I begged. 'Please look for me.'

When the nurse examined me, she was surprised. 'The head's right down there,' she said.

She took me straight to the delivery room and ten minutes later, I had my baby. 5.20 a.m. He was born blue, so they put him on the gas and air machine. He turned pink. Shane Dolan. 7lb-10. Born on Boxing Day.

It was the early hours of the morning. I sat crying and smoking in the room at the end of the maternity ward. I was shattered. I had been given 28 stitches and I ached. Where was Mick? I thought of telephoning my parents but it was too early. I did not want to wake them. I was desolate.

At 8.30 a.m. I telephoned Mum and Dad.

'I've got a little boy.'

'How was it?' Mum asked.

'I got through it,' I said, 'but I wouldn't want to do it again.'

'Are you all right? Do you need anything?'

'No. As soon as I get out, I'll come and see you and you can meet Shane.'

'Don't forget we love you,' Mum said. 'We're here if you need anything.'

At visiting time, the other new mums had their families around them – husbands, small children, flowers, chocolates and toys. Mick and his mum came at lunchtime – by then I was desperate to see him. He was all I had.

'Where were you last night?' I asked.

'My mates slipped me a Mickey Finn,' he said. 'I passed out.'

I knew he was lying, but I did not have the energy to pursue it. Maybe when he saw the baby, he would change.

Mick picked up Shane.

'Doesn't he look like me?' he said. 'I can't believe I've got a son.'

Mick left after half an hour and said he would be back that night. I waited for him, but he never showed up.

Before the birth, I was panicking, but as soon as I saw Shane I knew it would be all right. He had the most amazing blue eyes; they were like sapphires, so bright. I had to be shown how to feed him, bathe him, burp him – I was totally unprepared. I was nervous of him at first – he seemed so fragile – but I was overwhelmed by love.

On New Year's Eve, I was changing Shane's nappy. He was blue around the lips and the rest of his face was white and mottled.

'I think he might have a cold,' the Sister said. 'I'm going to ask the doctor to look at him.'

The doctor agreed Shane had a cold and took him up to intensive care.

'It's warmer up there,' he said. 'There's nothing to worry about.'

I gave Shane a cuddle. There was nothing to worry about so I was pleased he was going upstairs. I was totally exhausted. Now maybe I could sleep through the night.

I spent the evening in the day room with a pregnant woman and another whose child was in intensive care. We watched television and drank tea. At midnight we drank a glass of wine to welcome in the New Year, 1979.

The next morning, towards the end of breakfast, the consultant came into the day room and asked all the mothers to leave. I went towards the door, but he stopped me.

'Not you,' he said. 'It's you we want to see.'

The consultant held my hand. 'I'm afraid Shane's very poorly. He has a heart condition. We had to resuscitate him throughout the night.'

Shane was dying. My heart flew up to intensive care to be with him. My son was dying. I needed to be with him.

'We want to transfer him to the heart hospital in London, but we have to wait for him to stabilize.' The doctor was still holding my hand. 'I'm sorry,' he said. 'There is nothing else we can do. Do you want to go up and see him?'

'Yes,' I nodded. 'Yes, I do.'

Going up in the lift with the nurse, I was overwhelmed with guilt about the good time I had the night before. Drinking wine and seeing in the new year, while Shane was being resuscitated. Why did nobody tell me? They took him away and all I'd cared about was getting a good night's sleep.

The intensive care unit was massive and took up the top floor of the hospital. Shane was in a glass incubator, surrounded by lights and machines clicking and whirring. It looked like something out of a science fiction movie. Shane was naked except for a nappy. He had a tube up his nose and another coming from his ankle. He had monitors on his heart. I could see his breathing was laboured and slow.

'I'll leave you for a while,' the nurse said. 'I'll come back.'

I put my hands on the incubator walls and acknowledged that I had given birth. I looked at Shane's fingers, toes, eyes, ears, nose and I thought: 'This is my son, he is mine; he came from my body and it's up to me to look after him.' That is when the bond began – a bond that would last his entire life.

I was crying. Shane had to live – he had to. I willed it with every fibre of my being.

'Please don't let him die.'

I did not know who I was saying the words to. Shane opened his eyes. He had such bright eyes.

In that moment, I wanted God to exist, I wanted him to help me – help us. For the first time in my life I prayed.

'Please don't let Shane die. If you are really there,' I whispered, 'please, please don't let Shane die.'

5

I had to tell Mick. I went to the pay phone and dialled our number. Nine o'clock in the morning. There was no reply. I telephoned Mick's friend and his girlfriend answered the phone.

'Do you know where Mick is?' I asked her.

'No,' she said. 'I haven't seen him. But ...' she hesitated, '... I'm not sure whether to tell you, but I think you should know. While you've been in the hospital, Mick has been seeing Carol.'

Carol – the girl he had been seeing when I found out I was pregnant.

'Are you all right?' She sounded nervous.

She did not know Shane was ill – there was no point in telling her.

'Yes,' I said. 'It doesn't matter. I've got to go now.'

I put the telephone down. Mick was cheating on me again – somewhere inside me that hurt sat alongside the others, but I had no energy to be angry. My son was dying. I went back to intensive care and sat by Shane's incubator. I suddenly felt young and ignorant. I did not understand the equipment. I did not know what I was meant to do. I was vulnerable and scared and so very alone.

I did not telephone Mick's family. I thought of Mum, but I did not reach out to her either. I did not want to put my agony onto my family. I sat there with Shane, hour after hour.

That night I slept on the maternity ward. Every other mother was with her baby. I lay alone; the only mum without a crib by her bed. I was so lonely. My heart was being ripped apart. Would Shane live? Would I ever hold him again?

The next day, going up in the lift to be with Shane, I thought about God again – how much I wanted him to exist, despite all my feelings to the contrary. And I made a bargain with God.

'Please let Shane live and I promise I'll really try to be a good mum and a good person.'

On 3 January, Mick came to the hospital with his mum. I was so relieved to see him. He was six years older than me, I thought perhaps he would know what to do – maybe, with him there, it would be all right.

Mick stood at the incubator, his head bowed. He cried. 'Shane's dying, right?'

'Yes,' I said.

'I can't handle this,' Mick said.

I wanted to scream at him, 'I can't handle it either.'

I wanted Mick to take over, to be with me, but within 20 minutes he was gone.

I missed Mum. Everyone else had their parents, their children, their men. All the other new babies were welcomed into families. The ward was full of cards and toys and flowers that the visitors brought with them. Mick's mum gave me a tiny teddy bear and we put it at the bottom of Shane's incubator.

I was discharged from the hospital without Shane, to an unmarried mother's unit. It was an institution, not a home. There were eight rooms on my floor; sixteen people sharing one big kitchen. The bossy matron was harsh and unfeeling.

Shane had been in intensive care for a week when his doctor came to see me.

'We don't know how it is happening, but Shane is stabilizing and getting stronger,' he told me.

Better – Shane was getting better.

'This is the improvement we've been hoping for,' the doctor continued. 'Shane is well enough for us to arrange to take him to the Brompton Chest Hospital in London.'

We travelled to London in an ambulance. Shane – tiny in a portable incubator – relying on machinery to keep him alive. Would he make it? The ambulance team rolled the incubator through the Out Patients Department. There was a sense of urgency. Everyone was watching – I wanted to scream at them, 'He is not a freak show.'

Up in the lift, to the heart unit. Shane was whisked away from me; I was left alone. I lit a cigarette and looked out of the waiting room window. I was on my own, facing losing my son.

'Sis.'

I turned from the window. It was my brother.

'Pete, I can't believe you're here.'

Fifteen years old, he had bunked off school to be with me. In my moment of need, a member of my tribe had found me. I had never loved him more, never been so pleased to see anybody in my entire life.

'How's it going?'

'They're doing tests now, Pete, it's awful,' – I let myself tell him. 'Shane could die.'

Pete stayed the whole day. At 5 p.m. the doctor came to see us.

'Shane has a ventricular septral defect.'

'What does that mean?' My heart was pounding.

The doctor explained that there are four main chambers in the heart; Shane's top two had a hole in the wall between them. The oxygenated blood was getting mixed up with the non-oxygenated blood, so the oxygen in his blood was low.

'We'll put him on heart drugs,' the doctor said. 'We'll operate in a few months, when he is stronger.'

Shane was alive and there was hope. I began to think there might be a God and, if so, he might have listened to me. It was a comforting thought.

Pete wanted to come back with us to Ipswich.

'I don't want to leave you,' he said. 'What will you do on your own?'

I wanted – so wanted – him to come with us. I didn't want to lose his support. But the ambulance men said they could not carry another passenger. Pete stayed with us until the moment the ambulance drove off. My heart was breaking, but I knew I had to be strong.

For the first time, I could take Shane home – if you could call the mother and baby unit 'home'. It was an unsafe place, filled with people and kids running up and down and shouting.

For the first three days, I did not leave our tiny, cramped room.

I had bleached and disinfected everything – skirting boards, window panes, bed, cot, chest of drawers – before I brought Shane into it. But there were still dangers. Shane had been sent home with a warning: 'His immune system is very weak, don't let anyone who is ill go near him.' I was frightened to take Shane out of our room because of the risk of infection – and frightened to leave him alone in case he stopped breathing. I was always on red alert.

In addition, I had the responsibility of having to administer Shane's drugs. The hospital showed me how to put 0.05 milligrams on a dropper into his mouth twice a day. What if I got it wrong? There was a large skull and crossbones drawn on the bottle and the words 'Danger' and 'Poison'.

I barely slept, waking every hour to check Shane was still breathing. At 17, I was the youngest there. In the communal kitchen, the other mothers were laughing and joking, but I felt I had the world on my shoulders. I was too young, had a Southern accent and a very sick baby. Once again, I was an outsider.

Shane had not stopped crying for four hours. Something was wrong. He was sick. There was a telephone across the street – I had to get there. But I did not dare leave Shane alone in the room, nor take him outside. It was freezing; thick snow lay everywhere.

I knocked on my neighbour's door. She was 30 and looked glamorous and grown-up.

'Look after Shane for three minutes will you?' I asked, 'while I run across the road to phone the doctor?'

She shook her head.

'I can't,' she said. 'He's too sick. What if something happens while he's here with me?'

'I only want to make a phone call.'

'I'm really sorry,' she said. 'I can't handle the responsibility.'

I went back to my room. I was trapped. I don't know what I would have done if the health visitor had not turned up. It was her first visit since Shane and I got back from London and I wasn't expecting her.

She took one look at Shane, wrapped him in a blanket and said, 'Follow me to the hospital.'

She drove Shane away in her Mini and I walked through the snow to the hospital. I was wearing flip-flops and a cardigan. When I arrived at the hospital, I was wet and shaking from the cold. Shane was in an oxygen tent.

'It's just a precaution,' the doctor explained. 'He's got a bad cold. It's nothing for you to worry about.'

The knot that was my body began to unwind.

'Is he really out of danger?'

'Yes.' The doctor patted me on the shoulder. 'Have a break,' he said. 'Come back when he's feeling a bit better.'

I had no money and I had not eaten in three days. Luckily, I had my social security book on me and I went to the post office for some cash. Then I went around the corner to a café for breakfast.

A mug of steaming tea and hot buttered toast. For days all my senses had been taut; now someone else was looking after

Shane. For the first time, I relaxed a bit, felt like a girl again instead of a worn-down wreck.

Four days later, Shane came out of the oxygen tent.

'He's done so well,' the nurse said.

My heart swelled.

'Especially when you consider,' she continued matter-of-factly, 'that on Monday he nearly died.'

That was the day I was in the café. While I was drinking tea, my son was dying. No one had told me.

'But you said he was okay – he was out of danger.'

'I think the doctor thought you were a bit young to cope with knowing Shane had double pneumonia,' the nurse said. 'The doctor wanted to protect you.'

What made them think they had the right to decide what I should and shouldn't know? I was outraged – and filled with guilt.

'How long before I can take him home?'

'The doctor wants to talk to you about that.'

The doctor was brusque and officious.

'I'm very sorry Miss Dolan,' he said, 'but we don't think you have adequate provisions to look after Shane.'

'What do you mean?'

'Unless you can find somewhere more suitable to live, we can't release Shane from hospital.'

Somewhere else to live – my mind started racing.

'Have you considered adoption?'

'What?'

I looked at the doctor's eyes – he was serious.

'An older, more stable couple with more resources could give Shane a much better start in life' – he laid the plan out like a banquet – 'they could give Shane a safe future, a solid foundation.'

'But I haven't done anything wrong,' I tried to make him listen. 'I can learn,' I told him. 'I keep things clean.'

'It's not what you're doing,' the doctor said. 'It's where you live.'

There was no option. I had to find us somewhere else to live, but the local council would not help me. I had not been resident in the area long enough to qualify for housing. Landlords with private houses wanted hundreds of pounds in deposit and, when they learned I was on social security, they refused to consider me.

'Have you thought about adoption?' Each day when I went to the hospital, I was asked the same thing – by social workers, by nurses. 'There are people out there with houses and money; people who can take proper care of Shane. Don't be selfish. Think what's best for him.'

Something inside me knew absolutely that the best place for Shane was with me, his mother. To separate us would destroy something natural and right. I had to screen out the judgmental voices.

'You have one more week to find somewhere to live,' the doctor informed me. 'Shane can't stay in hospital any longer and you do not have a suitable place. The only alternative is foster care.'

I sat in the waiting room. I was desperate. Mum – if only I could call her. But I still felt I had to do it all on my own. Why?

What was I trying to prove? Suddenly the choice was clear: my child or my pride. Once I could see it, everything else fell into place.

I rang home.

'It's me – Mia.'

'All right, sis?' It was Jed. 'She's on the phone,' he called out.

Then everyone started to sing happy birthday. Suddenly I remembered – it was my birthday. I was 18 and I'd forgotten. I burst into tears. It was the first time I'd cried since that first day by the incubator.

'Mia.' It was Mum's voice. 'How have you been?'

She sounded familiar, concerned. My last reserve broke. I told her, 'Shane is really ill.'

'Come home,' Mum said. 'Bring him home.'

'Ask Dad' – I could not believe going home could be as easy as that.

'I don't have to ask your dad,' Mum said.

In the background I could hear him. 'Just tell the girl to come home' – his steady voice.

'Both of them – come home.'

When we pulled up outside my parents' house, the family bundled in the doorway to greet us: Mum, Dad, Peter, Jed. The first thing Mum said was, 'Let me hold Shane.'

It was the first time anyone other than medical staff had asked to do so. Everyone else had been terrified to go near him. I handed my son to my mother and she held him in one arm and put her other arm around me.

'You're home now Mia,' she said. 'Everything will be all right.'

Home: warm, cosy and safe. Sitting in the front room on the couch, Mum and I did a lot of talking. Her instinct about Mick had been right. She wanted to protect me from being hurt, but each person has to make their own mistakes.

I said, 'I was wrong to go to Ipswich.'

Mum said, 'I was wrong to try to stop you.'

Life took on a routine. While everyone was at work, I looked after Shane and the house and cooked a meal for when they came home. When Shane was three months old, I got a job working nights in a bar while he slept safely in my parents' house. It was exhausting but it was also good to be back in the world.

Mick always found a way to stay in touch, mostly by phone. Then he started to call more often. Something had changed.

'I miss you,' he said. 'I want to be with you and Shane.'

'It's not going to happen.' My answer was unequivocal. 'You had your chance. It's over now.'

A week later, Mick turned up at my parents' house. I was on my own with Shane. He strode in to the front room.

'If you don't want to get back together,' Mick said, 'then you're not keeping my son.'

I looked at him in amazement.

'I mean it,' he said. 'Get his stuff together – I'm taking him with me.'

In the kitchen, Mick picked up Shane's bottle and put it into his rucksack.

'Don't be ridiculous,' I said. 'You can't take Shane. You

don't know about his medication – you don't even know him.'

'I'll learn,' he said.

In that moment I realized Mick was serious. He thought he could walk in and take Shane from me. All I could think about was Shane's safety. I couldn't leave him alone with Mick, he had no idea about real life. He did not know what it took to keep Shane alive: having to administer the drugs so carefully. He'd never spent an hour alone with his son, and now he thought he could take care of him.

I heard a buzzing in my ears – the same sound I heard the day I fought back against the fifth formers at school. Mick turned his back to pick up Shane's milk formula, and I grabbed the bread knife that was lying by the sink.

Mick turned and I held the knife up.

'You're not taking Shane,' I said.

Mick looked at me scornfully.

'You haven't got the guts,' he said.

He moved towards me and I lifted the knife. He moved sideways and I brought the blade down through his coat, pinning him to the back door.

'Fucking hell' – Mick was breathless. 'You're mad.'

He dropped the bag filled with all the things Shane depended on. I put my foot on the door and used my weight to pull the knife out of Mick's coat.

'Get the fuck out of this house,' I said.

I did not see him again for seven years.

I spent my days with Shane and my nights working at Woody's bar: life was repetitive and sane. I loved living with Mum and

Dad again. I was sharing a house with my best friends. They were strong in their support of Shane – two other pairs of eyes to watch over his health and medication. I felt safe and loved and secure again.

Dark hair, green eyes, 6-ft tall – Andy was an old school friend of my brother Jed. He asked me out for the evening and we played pool and talked. He was very relaxed and easy going.

A week later, I was rushed into hospital with appendicitis. Andy came to visit with gifts: perfume, flowers, cosmetics, chocolates – even a hairbrush. He was there all the time.

When I got home, he came to see me every day. He was good with Shane. One night we went to the park and he told me about his childhood. His stepfather was a bully; Andy never felt loved by him. He said his mother was caught in the middle and ended up letting him down. He looked at our family, he said, and it made him want to have one of his own.

'If we get together,' he said, 'I'll make sure nothing bad ever happens to Shane.'

Shane was a year old. It would be wonderful for him to have a father. I liked to hear Andy speak.

'Will you live with me?' Andy asked.

We sat in silence. I thought about Mick – how tortuous living with him had been.

'No,' I said at last. 'There's no security in that.'

'Let's get married then,' he said.

'Married?'

It sounded romantic but … 'There's so much to organize,' I said, trying to sound practical.

'We can do it quickly.'

'How quickly?'

Andy was on a roll.

'Let's see how quickly,' he said. 'It will be a laugh.'

There was no great romance; we had been going out for four weeks. We kept it a secret in case anyone tried to stop us. Andy paid for a special licence. He was right – it was fun.

The night before we got married, Mum found out. She tried to talk to me.

'Do you know what you're doing?' she asked.

'Yes,' I said. 'Andy is going to be a good father to Shane.'

'And you?'

'He'll be good to me too.'

Mum knew better than to say, 'Don't'; she looked defeated.

'Andy had a bad childhood,' I tried to reassure her, 'and he wants a chance to do it differently.'

The next day, Mum looked after Shane, while Andy and I drove to the registry office in Sittingbourne. We sat on plastic chairs in the waiting room. I was wearing a cream and rust-coloured silk shirt and silky cream trousers; Andy was wearing a cream-coloured v-neck t-shirt.

The ceremony was over in 15 minutes. It would have taken longer to get a haircut. Driving back to the island over Kingsferry Bridge, it hit me. I was married to the stranger next to me. What had I done?

When we got back to the house to pick up Shane, Jed and Pete opened the door.

'Sneaky sods,' they said. 'You don't get away with it that easily.'

The hallway was filled with friends and family. There were balloons in the kitchen. Mum had organized a surprise celebration party for us. There was even a small wedding cake.

Andy pulled me aside.

'I want to go,' he said.

'We can't,' I told him. 'We've just got here – and look at all the trouble Mum's gone to.'

'I don't feel right,' Andy said. 'I want to go.'

I made our excuses and mum filled a Tupperware box with bits and pieces from the buffet. She hugged me hard.

'Be happy,' she said.

Then, leaving Shane with Mum for the night, we set off for Leysdown – our new life in a chalet, three miles away. The chalet was so cold, we went straight to bed and stayed there until the next day – with our Tupperware box of buffet bits and a bottle of Mum's best brandy. We made love, talked, drank, ate. We laughed a lot.

Andy apologized for dragging me away from the party and I told him it was fine. He was the first man with whom I had an orgasm. I thought that was love.

We had been married for three months when I found out I was pregnant. I was horrified.

'I don't want any more children,' I told Andy. 'What if the child is born with a birth defect? What if it's worse than Shane's?'

'It won't be.' Andy tried to soothe me. He was excited at

the prospect of becoming a father. 'It's great news, Mia,' he enthused. 'It's perfect.'

Andy liked the fantasy of being a father, but the practicalities escaped him. We had to move into emergency council accommodation. Andy, Shane and I in one room; we lived surrounded by dustbin bags filled with our possessions.

We had been there three weeks when, one morning, there was blood running down my legs. Andy called an ambulance. We raced through the streets, siren blaring. Up until that moment, I had not wanted to be pregnant but now, suddenly, this baby was precious to me. I did not want to lose my baby.

'If you are there God,' – I reached out as I had when I was about to lose Shane – 'let me keep this baby.'

By the time we arrived at the hospital, the bleeding had stopped. Two days later, I went home.

When I was five months pregnant, we got our first house; an old coastguard cottage. It was run-down and dingy but it felt like our first step towards respectability and parenthood. We painted and carpeted the whole place and filled it with second-hand furniture.

'She's perfect.'

Minutes old, our new baby girl was wrapped in a blanket in Andy's arms. He had tears in his eyes.

'Truly?' I asked him.

'Truly.'

This time, my baby's father was there – but I could not enjoy the moment, I could not relax.

'What's her colour like?'

'Pink.'

'Check her heart,' I begged the nurse.

'What's the matter with you?' the nurse was sharp. 'She's a perfect little girl.'

On the maternity ward, Tanya was laid in a crib beside me. She had turquoise eyes and soft dark hair. The doctor came to see us. He told me that while I had been pushing Tanya out of my body, he had noticed a growth coming from my urethra.

'We'll have to operate in the next couple of days.'

I barely heard him.

'When you've finished the examination,' – it was all I cared about – 'will you check my daughter's heart?'

Reluctantly, he listened to her chest with a stethoscope.

'She's fine, Mrs Ogilvie,' he said.

But I was not reassured. Deep in my heart I believed Tanya had a heart condition. At any moment, she would die. I was afraid to get close to her; I held her only to feed or change her – never for a cuddle. This was not going to hurt me.

On the third day, Shane's doctor came to see us. At last, here was someone who would take my fears seriously. She had always told me the truth. She spent 20 minutes examining Tanya. Then she wrapped her back up in her blanket. I held my breath. She smiled.

'You've got a perfectly healthy baby girl,' she said.

When the doctor had gone, I picked Tanya up. I spent the next hours holding her close to my body and looking – really looking – at her. It was the first time I allowed myself to feel for my child. I felt a surge of love – a wave that rolled over me and carried me with it.

Tanya was 10 days old. I had no fear about my operation – it was a formality, a little cut. Then I could go home and be with my new family. All my sights were set on that.

I came around in a little side room. There was a bed, a buzzer and a clock. I was alone. I tried to sit up, but I could not move. I tried to move my legs. Nothing at all. Legs, feet, toes, hips – nothing moved. I could not feel anything from my ribs down. Using my arms, I pulled myself across the bed to the buzzer. The nurse came in.

'Something's happened.' I could hear panic in my voice. 'I can't feel my legs.'

The nurse took my pulse.

'It's nothing to worry about,' she said. 'You're feeling a bit strange because of the anaesthetic.'

'I can't feel anything,' I said. 'I can't move. Please look. Please sort it out.'

She pulled the blankets up and pinched my toe.

'Can you feel that?'

I could see her touching my foot, but I could not feel any-thing. I started to cry.

'I can't feel anything. I can't move.'

She pinched the toe on my other foot.

'No,' I said again. 'Nothing.'

'Don't worry' – her tone did not change – 'anaesthetics can be funny things. I'll get the doctor to come and talk to you.'

The doctor had a nappy pin. He pressed it into my thigh. Nothing.

'This?' – he pressed it into my foot.

I looked into his eyes. 'No.'

'Squeeze my finger.'

I managed that.

'We'll run some tests,' the doctor said. 'It's nothing to worry about. We'll sort it out.'

The hours that followed were the longest of my life. I was left alone in the room with the door shut. Outside the window, an overgrown bush rattled against the glass. My gaze went between the clock and the window, the window and the clock, the whole night. I thought: 'This is it, for the rest of my life, propped up in a bed unable to move.' I had two tiny children. What was I going to do?

In all the difficult situations in my life, I had been pro-active. That was what had got me through – making decisions, doing things. Now I was totally helpless. Totally vulnerable. I could not do anything. I could not even get to the door.

Around 6 a.m., I began to feel a tingling in my legs. Pins and needles. Sensation. Relief. Feet on the floor, I wobbled – one foot careful, careful, then the other – across the floor to the door, holding on to the wall.

For months afterwards, I would be in the middle of washing a cup or feeding a child and, suddenly, my legs would go numb. I never knew when – or if – the feeling would come back. The hospital arranged for me to have home help.

I wanted someone to say sorry. I went to a solicitor for advice and it turned out I had a case for medical negligence. It took years for the truth to emerge: in the pre-operation room, a junior anaesthetist mistook me for another patient and gave me an epidural – he also put it in the wrong place. He put a hugely powerful anaesthetic intended for the spine into my sacroid space – and he administered far too much of it. Over the years, as the facts came out, I was more and more shocked by the treatment I received.

Tanya was three months old. I asked Andy to look after the children so I could go to bingo with Mum.

'I haven't had a night out since Tanya was born,' I reasoned.

Andy was nervous.

'If you get the kids to sleep before you go, I'll do it,' he bargained.

I was gone for two hours. When I came home, the house was in chaos, both children were screaming.

'I'm never doing that again,' Andy said.

He was true to his word. In all the years we were married, he never once allowed me to leave the children alone with him. But he made up for it in other ways. He was a good provider. We always had enough to eat and the children had everything they needed. He was being a father the best way he could – but his business kept him out a lot. Buying and selling cars, he said.

One afternoon Pete came to see me.

'I've got to tell you something,' he said.

We sat at the kitchen table. I made two mugs of tea but Pete did not touch his. Instead, he kept jumping up from his chair and pacing the room.

'I don't want to hurt you,' he began. 'I've been up all night asking myself what to do.'

My heart began to hammer.

'I was round at Mark's house last night and Andy was there with a girl on his lap.'

'What were they doing?'

'They were kissing.'

Pete was looking at me, trying to gauge my reaction.

'I didn't want to tell you but I thought you'd want to know.'

'Who is she?'

'Joy.'

Joy was a friend; Shane played with her little boy.

'I'll sort it out Pete. You were right to tell me.'

To be so casual in front of my brother, the relationship with Joy must have been going on for a while. But how long? And how had I not known about it? Just the night before, Andy and I made love. I loved him. I thought he loved me.

Betrayal. The pain of rejection. I had allowed myself to trust a man and again I'd been let down. I felt angry at myself for being so trusting. But most of all I raged at Andy.

I filled a suitcase with his clothes. When he opened the front door, I was standing at the top of the stairs.

'You bastard.'

I threw the case down from the top of the stairs; it hit him on the chest and knocked him backwards.

'I know about you and Joy,' I said. 'Get out.'

'I'm not going anywhere,' Andy said. 'This is my house as much as yours.'

He walked into the front room and sat down on the couch.

'Right,' I said. 'I'll go.'

6

I trusted Andy and he'd betrayed me. I felt I'd been kicked all over. I went to Mum and Dad's house. I was climbing the wall – I had to get out. I telephoned Jed's wife Theresa and then my friend Janet.

'Let's get hammered,' I said.

I had not been out with my friends since the day I married Andy – 14 long months. I wanted to blot out the pain.

We went on a pub crawl along Sheerness High Street. I was drinking alcohol like lemonade, but thoughts of Andy and the way he lied to me still gnawed at my insides.

We walked into our seventh pub, The Crown, and I noticed a friend of Pete's at the bar. I had known Alan for years, he was often in my parents' house. As we spoke, I found myself thinking: 'I could sleep with you.' I wanted to burn every memory of Andy from my body.

I could sleep with him – in my mind I began to contemplate the practicalities – how, where – and then a girl I knew came out of the toilets and sat in the empty stool on Alan's other side.

'Do you know my girlfriend, Tracey?' Alan asked.

I was a double fool. I had never had a one-night stand in my life – what was I thinking of? I ordered a taxi to take me back to Mum and Dad's. There was no escape – nothing to take the pain away.

The next day, Andy came round.

'Can we talk?' he asked.

We sat on the wall outside the house.

'Joy has been coming on to me and I did like the attention,' he admitted. 'But I didn't take it any further. I wouldn't do anything to ruin our family.'

He had tears in his eyes. 'I promise I'll be more considerate,' he said. 'Please come back.'

I didn't believe him, but I had two young children. I thought perhaps we could sort it out; make it work somehow.

'All right,' I said, 'but if it happens again, we're finished.'

I went home with him that morning and life picked up where it had broken off. The children were safe and happy; I told myself I had made the sensible choice. Three days after my return, we were sitting watching television and I looked across at Andy and I knew it: the passion I had felt for him was finished. I was no longer in love with him.

I'd had two children unplanned. When I fell pregnant with Shane I was on the pill – and with Tanya I'd been told I couldn't get pregnant. With my track record, I could have 10 kids by the time I was 30. I loved them both to bits, but I absolutely knew I didn't want any more children.

I went to see my doctor and told him I wanted to be sterilized. I was 21 years old. Too young – he assumed – to make such a decision. He arranged for me to be interviewed by a panel of doctors.

'What if your husband should die or you should separate and meet someone else? Then you would want more children,' the doctor persisted, 'wouldn't you?'

'Are you saying that every time I say, "I love you," I have to produce a child to prove it?'

The vehemence of my answer won the day. Three weeks later, I was sterilized.

From the moment Shane was born, I'd been told he'd have to have an operation on his heart. But four years on, the doctors took him off his medication.

'I'm not sure quite how it happened,' the young doctor told me truthfully, 'but Shane has made an unprecedented recovery. He won't need the heart operation after all.'

I had been warned that Shane would always be thin, weak and lacking in energy, but nothing could have been further from the truth. At the age of four, Shane was big, solid – and terrifyingly hyperactive.

When Tanya was 18 months old, Andy's hepatitis flared up and he became very ill. We lived on sickness benefit and money was tight. I was looking after Andy and he resented it. He wanted to be the strong one, the breadwinner; he saw that as his role.

Any money I spent had to be accounted for to the penny and I had to show him the receipts. He found the children too noisy. I did my best to keep the peace: I kept the house clean and tidy, took Shane and Tanya out to give him space.

'Look at the state of this place,' he said one morning, running his hand along the top of the front room door. There was dust – he found it and waved it at me. I got a duster and cleaned the door. Andy never lifted a finger in the house, but he loved to complain.

The first time someone criticizes you, it hurts; you want to do better. The next time and the time after, you feel the attack, but after that you just take it for granted. I tiptoed around him, working hard at doing the things that made life run smoothly: a tidy house, buying foods I thought Andy liked to eat, cooking proper meals and serving them on time. Lunch at one o'clock; dinner on the dot of seven.

It had all started when Tanya was born. Andy was fearfully protective of her. He wouldn't allow guests to see her if he thought they had a cold. Everything had to be perfect for his daughter, but he didn't feel the same about Shane. Tanya had his heart and Shane did not.

It hurt me to feel Shane was overlooked; he needed a dad – Andy had promised to be one. When guests came to the house, Andy always praised Tanya. He would go on and on about how wonderful she was. He never mentioned Shane.

One lunchtime, I cooked mashed potatoes.

'There's lumps in this,' Andy said.

He threw the dinner plate at the wall; it landed inches from my head. There was a mess of potato, meat and gravy over the wallpaper.

The children were silent.

'All I want is to eat proper food,' Andy roared. 'I'm ill and you don't give a shit.'

I grabbed the children's coats and took them to the beach. The tide was out and we wandered along the pebbles looking for crabs. We had no toys and no money.

I thought about the dinner and I thought about Andy's reaction; hard as I tried I couldn't see a reason for his violent explosion. I did not know what I had done. It was the first time Andy scared me.

I started off thinking I would never go back – this was the end. But by teatime, we were tired and hungry. I went to a pay phone and reversed the charges.

'It's me.'

Andy asked, 'Where are you?'

'At the beach with the kids.'

There was silence.

'Don't you think you over-reacted?' Andy said. 'You didn't have to leave.'

'You scared the life out of me.'

'I just lost my temper,' Andy said. 'I didn't hurt anybody.'

'If I come back, is it going to be all right?'

'Of course,' Andy said. 'Come home.'

Outside the phone box, waiting for Andy to pick us up, I explained to the children, 'Dad said he's really sorry he had a tantrum. He wants us to go home and have tea.'

Later that night, when the children were in bed, I sat on the sofa beside Andy.

'We need to talk about this,' I said. 'You scared me – and you scared the kids.'

'I've been feeling really ill,' Andy said. 'And I'm freaked out about money. I just seemed to lose it.'

Andy was sorry. He made me a promise.

'I will never hurt you or the children,' he said.

It was in this midst of this that things started to disappear.

It began with Andy's glasses. He always left them at the side of the bed when he went to sleep. One morning, we woke and they were gone. We combed the house from top to bottom. We even upended the bed and looked underneath. Andy was grumpy. He needed his glasses.

'I don't understand it,' he said over again.

I tidied the house as usual and made the beds. There was no sign of Andy's glasses until late afternoon, when I went into our bedroom to get a jumper and there they were – right in the centre of our duvet.

It was Tanya's hairbrush next. She had long blonde hair and I always kept the brush in the kitchen so I could tidy her up before she left the house. The same thing happened: the brush went missing and then turned up in the middle of an empty coffee table.

Objects disappeared so many times, I got to the stage where I just trusted they would turn up, eventually, in a very obvious place. I didn't think about the weirdness – I didn't want to. It's only looking back I realize this was the beginning of my paranormal experiences.

It started with the lost objects and then, one night, the bed shook so violently I woke up. This became a regular occurrence, along with the TV changing channels by itself and the lights switching themselves on and off.

It was at this point that I first heard the voice.

I went to the doctor and told him about the bed and the TV and the lights.

'It's stress,' he said. 'When you're anxious you tremble, that explains the movement in the bed.'

'And the electrical stuff?'

'It's just forgetfulness. Everything you have described to me is stress related.'

I had a recurring nightmare. I was walking through a valley – a green bowl between two hills – and as I walked, a black mist came down. I had to get myself out, but the mist had fingers that clawed me down, pulling me under. I woke up sweating, my heart racing.

One night when I was struggling to climb out of the mist, I raised my hands to the sky. In the dream, light came out of the sky and went into my hands, through my entire body and out round my feet. The light broke up the mist. It was the most amazing feeling, seeing the light take the darkness away.

I woke at 4 a.m., got out of bed and went downstairs for a cup of tea and a cigarette. I felt very peaceful. I knew I would not have the dream again. Something important was finished. I felt linked to something bigger than myself.

Then the real turning point came. The Sunday morning when, hanging out the washing, I found myself transported to the scene of a horrific plane crash that had not yet happened. It gave me proof that all these strange occurrences were not my imagination – or stress-related or madness. I didn't want to believe it, but this stuff was real. Something was happening to me and I wanted it to stop.

The day after the plane crash, Mum and I scoured *The Yellow Pages* and the local paper. We looked up 'ghosts', 'paranormal' and 'psychic' before eventually looking up 'spirit' and finding 'Spiritualist Church'.

I telephoned the Spiritualist Church in Sheerness.

'Can you help people who have weird things going on?' I asked.

'Yes dear.' The woman on the other end of the line sounded mumsy and friendly. 'Come along to the church,' she said.

Church – the word was off-putting. I had no idea what was in store. Was the room going to be filled with hippies? Would everyone be dressed in black and chanting? But I felt better after talking to the woman. I felt like someone with a rare disease who suddenly finds a specialist. I was about to meet people who knew what I was going through; people who would not be phased by it.

There was a meeting at the church that night. Mum came over to babysit (even though Andy was in the house). I arrived late at the church and slipped into a chair in the back row. I was in the Labour Party Hall, surrounded mostly by women – all respectable looking in twin sets and comfortable shoes. What was I doing here?

I was brought up to be a Catholic and, at first sight, this looked like paganism. At the top of aisle there was a Formica table covered with a blue velvet cloth. I could see a silver crucifix on a stand and a bible.

'We will start with a hymn. You will find your hymn books by your chairs.'

This was getting worse – just like a proper church. They sang 'Onward Christian Soldiers'; I mouthed the words, all the time cringing. What if any of my friends knew that I had come here?

'Dear Lord,' a woman said as the song came to a close. 'Thank you for your blessings in letting us gather here tonight. Keep us under your protection so we can link with loved ones in safety. Amen.'

'Amen.'

The medium was a man in a dark suit; he was about 60 with a bald head and round face. He had very bushy eyebrows. He spoke for a few minutes about lessons in life and how to think of others. Then he closed his eyes, opened them and started speaking to a woman at the back of the room. Her late husband, he said, had a message for her. I thought it was rubbish – preying on her hope and naiveté. And anyway, it wasn't what I was looking for. I was looking for someone to take away the voice, not encourage it.

'You have powerful colours,' the medium said.

He was walking down the aisle towards me.

'You have the colours of a natural earth medium,' he said. 'You have a gift.'

My heart was pounding.

'Try to keep a handle on it,' he said. 'You're a bit young for this. It will be out of your control. Be careful.'

Then he was gone, moving on to the next person.

At the end, I stayed around while they served tea in china

cups and custard creams on saucers. I wanted to talk to the medium but I was told he was exhausted. He did not appear.

Although I was cynical, the medium's words had given me hope. I wanted the weird things to stop and this was the closest thing I had to an answer. So every week, for the next two months, I skulked at the back of the Labour Hall, listening to mediums. I was very sceptical, but it was exciting when the psychics got it right. One medium told a member of the audience where her late husband had his savings; another knew the last words a dying mother spoke.

It was the end of my sixth meeting and, along with the tea and biscuits, we were offered a session with a healer. We formed a queue. I had no idea what healing was, but it was my first chance to have a one-to-one with somebody who might be able to help me. I was determined to make her take the voice away.

The healer was in her mid-fifties, with short brown hair. She was wearing a lemon-coloured cardigan. Members of the audience sat in the chair in front of her and she put her hands around their heads. I noticed a fuzzy glow around her shoulders. I looked around the hall, trying to find where the light came from. (I now know I was seeing my first aura – an energy field which people don't usually see.)

It was my turn. I sat in the chair with my back towards the healer and, without touching, she put her hands around my head. I could feel the heat from her hands even though they were inches from my head. Then my shoulders dropped. I had not realized I was so tense.

'There's a lot of activity around you,' I heard her say. 'So much energy. You're having a frightening time.'

Suddenly I was telling her everything – it was all tumbling out in a great torrent of words: the voice, the lights, the plane crash. Throughout, she kept moving her hands around my head and shoulders.

'Do you think you can take it away?' I asked.

'You have a gift,' the healer said. 'It's only scaring you because you don't understand. You need to know how to control it.'

'Yes, yes,' I said impatiently. 'But can you get rid of it?'

'You are unusually young to be so open,' she said, 'but no – you can't get rid of it.'

Despair. This voice – these weird things – would never go away. I felt trapped.

She told me, 'The voice you can hear is your guide.'

What was she on about?

'He is trying to talk to you,' she said. 'He's not the bogeyman; he has your best interests at heart.'

She was talking about the voice as if it was a person. I was irritated, but at the same time intrigued. Something in her matter-of-fact tone made me listen.

'Your guide can help you develop your gift. He's there to help you help others. Talk to him. I can't take the voice away, but I can stop you being frightened,' the healer said. 'I'll show you a visualization technique so you'll be able to shut down when you want to.'

The technique involved visualizing a stage with curtains closing.

'I just visualize that and it's going to stop?' I asked incredulously.

She squeezed my shoulders.

'Be patient and you'll see.'

Outside the hall, I lit a cigarette and went over all she had said. I walked home along the High Street. Everything looked the same but I felt different. I felt she had given me a spell.

Before I could shut down, it seemed, I had to talk to my guide.

'Are you there?' I said. I was trying it out – I did not expect an answer.

'Yes.'

The voice sounded bored but gentle. It was the first time I had instigated a conversation and I had got an immediate response. Oh shit. I took another drag on my cigarette.

At Catholic school I had been taught that everyone has a guardian angel; occasionally they spoke to saints and prophets. But I had a husband on sickness benefit and I spent my whole day looking after children – I was hardly the sort of person angels came to talk to. I didn't even believe in God.

'Okay,' I said. 'Okay, if you're real, why me? I don't believe in God, and I'm not a particularly good person.'

There was no answer, so I carried on, talking to the sky.

'Why not pick on a nun or someone spiritual?'

The answer, when it came, was dry.

'Your guess,' it said, 'is as good as mine.'

7

If I was going to be talking to a voice as if it was real, the first thing I wanted to know was whether it was there in my private moments. Back at home in my lounge, I said aloud, 'Do you watch me when I'm in bed?'

I knew my question was inane, but I had to ask.

'Do you watch me in the bath?'

'No,' the voice said each time.

'And when I had sex the other night?'

'No.' The tone was kind but disinterested.

'I'm just asking. It's important. Do you know what I'm doing all the time?'

'Yes.'

I began to wish I had never started the conversation. I wanted normality. I turned on the television.

But I could not stop thinking about the voice. A few nights later, when Andy was out and the children were in bed, I decided to see if it was still around. I was in the kitchen, washing the dishes.

'Are you still here?' I said into the air.

'Yes.'

The voice came from outside my head, clear, close, real. Was he standing there?

'Can anyone else hear you?' I asked.

'No, it's only you I talk to.'

'You won't frighten the children, will you?'

'I've no desire to frighten anyone.'

The tone was slightly impatient. I went into the front room and turned the television on, but I could not concentrate. I was in turmoil. Speaking to the voice was so weird – it couldn't be real – and yet it felt as real as anything else in my life.

I had started something, but I was scared to carry on. I felt like running from my house – as if it was haunted. But the ghost – or whatever it was – was not with the house, it was with me. There was nowhere to go.

I tried to watch a TV programme, then I wandered upstairs to check on the children. I did not know what to do with myself. Back in the lounge, I sat down and turned the television off. There must be some reason why the voice had turned up. I decided to find out what it was.

'Okay,' I said aloud. 'What do you want?'

'I believe we're meant to work together.'

'Work?' I asked. 'What work? Doing what?'

'That's up to you.'

'That's ridiculous,' I said. 'I don't even believe in God.'

I waited for an answer, but nothing came back. So I asked him the biggest question I could think of.

'Is there a God?'

The answer was immediate. 'Yes.'

I lit a cigarette. Up to that point I had been hesitant and

nervous, now suddenly I was angry. If there was a God, why was there so much suffering in the world? All my unanswered questions tumbled into my head. I'd been fed all this God stuff as a child and never been shown anything to back it up. The world was full of atrocities. I was filled with resentment and ready for a fight.

'Okay,' I said. 'If there's a God, why does he let children get hurt? Why does he let people starve? What about disease and famine and earthquakes?'

I was pacing the room. I went on and on, itemising the pains of the world until I ran out of breath. When I had finished, I sat down.

'Why?' I asked again.

'God doesn't make bad things happen,' the voice said. 'Just as he doesn't make good things happen.'

'That's a cop out,' I said.

'Imagine you have a child who is autistic,' the voice said. 'The child is isolated, lost in its own world. Now imagine a doctor says, "Give me your child for one year and he will return healed. But while he's away he will have to suffer. But if you do not give me your child then, forever, he will be isolated and alone." Would you let your child go?'

'Well, of course I'd give the child.'

'As God sends you to Earth,' the voice said.

The words made sense to me. My anger fell away. In my early teens, I'd looked at the Church and seen its hypocrisy. I came to the conclusion that God didn't exist. Now I was left with a deep understanding. It was so obvious, so simple. It wasn't personal.

It wasn't 'God's will'. Good and bad luck were random.

Over the following months, I came to know a lot about what my guide thought. I became very interested in the things he had to say. He had a perspective which was very calming and helped me see the world with more understanding. Instead of fighting against life, I seemed to be in tune with it. I felt that the voice was my teacher.

'So life is like school?' I asked him.

'Yes.'

'Then why do some people have a really bad time and others seem to float through life?'

'They are having harder lessons,' the voice said. 'They are older spirits, they have been around longer.'

'What do you mean?'

'An older spirit – one who has been on earth a number of times and already experienced many emotions – has the ability to deal with the harder lessons of life,' he said. 'A young spirit does not have the capacity to deal with a lot of pain and so he may crack.

'The spirit can only grow through emotional experiences,' the voice told me. 'The more painful the emotion, the more knowledgeable the spirit becomes. Ultimately, the main aim is to experience all there is to experience.'

I put my hand in the air.

'I don't want to talk anymore,' I said.

The voice stopped. It did not impose itself. Alone in the house, I tapped into the ability I had nurtured in childhood to switch off when things got too much. I made a cup of tea and turned on the television. I did not want to think about it anymore.

I wanted to say to people, 'I know the answers – I know why we're here.' But the answers I had were so obvious I could have come up with them myself. Sometimes I wondered if that was the truth. Part of me still did not believe what I was experiencing. I still had moments when I thought I was quite mad – and was terrified anyone else would find out that I spoke to an invisible man.

Yet as long as I kept my conversations with the voice a secret, I reasoned, there was no harm in finding out more. My fear was dissipating – and my curiosity was growing. It was like having a new playmate; I wanted to test it out and see what I could do with it.

Sitting on the couch in the front room, I tried again. I was feeling excited and happy, I was looking forward to talking to the voice.

'Are you there?'

There was no reply. I felt a slightly panicky sense of disappointment. What if he had gone? What if it was all over?

'Are you there? Are you there?'

'Yes.'

'Have you got a name?'

'Merlin.'

Merlin – that threw me totally. 'No way,' I said. It was ludicrous. 'I suppose you've got King Arthur there with you,' I said sarcastically, 'and the Round Table.'

There was no reply.

'I'm not doing Merlin,' I said.

There was a pause and then the voice said, 'How about Eric?'

'Eric,' I said, relieved. That was an ordinary, sensible name. 'Okay,' I said, 'Eric. But I don't want to hear the name Merlin again.'

I had been formulating questions in the days since we last spoke. I got scared when he spoke of reincarnation, but now I was ready to find out more.

'Is there a hell?'

'No,' he said, 'not as you understand it.'

'So everyone goes to heaven?'

'There are different levels of ...' he paused and then placed a gentle emphasis on the word 'heaven' – using my (rather than his) word for it.

'So when you die, you get judged and go to your level?' I said.

'You judge yourself.'

'Yeah, but everyone will judge themselves well,' I said, 'to go to a high level.'

'No,' Eric said. 'You are judged by your higher self.'

'Oh, so there's two of me,' I said. 'I've got a lower and higher self – like a twin sister, only better.'

'You are your higher self and your lower self,' Eric said. 'While you are on Earth, only your lower self is awake.'

'Is it the same as having a guilty conscience?' I asked. 'When you know you've done something you shouldn't and it nags at you – is it like that?'

'Similar.'

'Well, that could be hell then,' I concluded.

I had the feeling that Eric had a limited amount of energy and time, so I raced on.

'So we're going to work together?'

'Yes.'

'What are we going to do?'

'We're going to help people.'

'Okay, how?'

'By giving them understanding and knowledge.'

I thought about the day I told Jennifer she was pregnant and my awareness that Janet and Will were splitting up. I had a magical ghost and all I had to do was ask him questions. The possibilities were endless.

'So I'll be able to meet people and you'll tell me all about their lives,' I said excitedly, 'what they've been through, where they're going and then I'll be able to tell them.'

'It can't work like that,' Eric said. 'You've got to learn how to see.'

'How do I learn to see?'

'You just have to learn how to look.'

'Can I get any books on this?'

'You don't need books,' he said. 'All the information you need is inside you.'

I could hear Shane upstairs, beginning to cry.

I felt disappointed and deflated. The initial excitement had worn off. I couldn't use Eric as a party trick to impress my friends. It wasn't all going to be given to me in one go. I had to somehow understand – and it would take effort.

I had the impression I needed to be trained in some way

but I was not sure I wanted to do the work involved. Apart from the voice, the only thing I'd actually seen was the plane crash. I didn't want to see images like that again.

Besides, life was busy; almost every minute was taken up with Andy and the children, school, cooking and cleaning. Andy was still at home: unwell, irritable and refusing to help out with anything domestic. Where was I going to find the time and patience to study with a ghostly angel? And for what – so that at some time in the future, I could stand in a spiritualist church and put my hands around someone's head? It seemed pointless.

'I've been thinking about all of this,' I told Eric the next time I was alone, 'and I really can't see myself as knowledgeable Mother Earth. I'd find this whole thing much easier to grasp if I could see you. Is that possible? Can you let me see you?'

'You're not ready yet,' he said.

'So I'm ready to hear a voice talking out of the air,' I said, 'but not ready to see the person behind the voice.'

'No,' Eric replied. 'You're not ready.'

'I haven't reached a decision yet,' I told him. 'I don't know whether you're real or I'm mad. It would help me to see you.'

'So be it,' Eric said.

The door leading from the front room to the hall was open. I watched a tiny curl of mist appear in the doorway. The mist solidified into a light which grew stronger and brighter. It suddenly stretched from the top of the frame to the carpet, then the light parted like a curtain and a man was standing there.

He was an old man; about 5-ft-7. He was wearing a brown robe, like a monk's habit, with stains down the front of it. He had leather sandals on his feet. Most of his head was bald, but he had hair around the sides. He had very blue eyes.

His hands were resting on a gnarled walking stick; they looked twisted and swollen. Eric was leaning slightly forward and he looked at me with a very gentle smile.

I shot back in my chair, gabbling, 'Oh my God, you're right, I'm not ready. I'm not ready.'

The curtain of light closed, leaving a thin column of light. The column shrunk to a small disc, which glowed for a moment, then disappeared. Terrified, I telephoned Mum and she came over and stayed with me until Andy got home.

From paintings in cathedrals and churches, I had been expecting a Charlton Heston lookalike wearing glowing white robes. I was ready to see a heavenly body. The last thing I expected was to discover my guardian angel was past his sell-by date and wearing grubby clothes. My angel – to my chagrin – was old and decrepit.

'I thought he might appear as a shadowy mist,' I told Mum. 'Or an angel with wings in shimmering light. But to see an old man in my doorway – that was more scary than anything I could have imagined.'

'You asked to see him,' Mum tried to comfort me. 'He said you weren't ready, but you insisted. He won't show himself unless you ask him to.' Mum, in her intuitive way, seemed to have more faith in Eric than I did. 'He's on your side,' she said.

A few nights later in bed, Andy rolled onto his side and was immediately asleep. I lay beside him, thinking about Eric. It was clear he wanted everything on his own terms; we had to do it his way. It was not the scenario I had in mind at all, but I still wanted to interact.

I did not want to speak out loud for fear I might wake Andy so, for the first time, I tried to reach Eric by calling for him inside my head.

'Eric, can you hear me?'

'Yes.'

Up till then I had always heard Eric outside of me, but this time the answer was inside my head. Our connection felt suddenly cosy, intimate. I was not alone, he was always with me.

'So what do I do?' I asked.

'Relax,' Eric instructed. 'Close your eyes and drift, without going to sleep. Observe the images you get without emotion.'

I closed my eyes and waited. After a few moments, I saw three pebbles lying next to each other. I got excited and the picture went. I tried again. Every time, I felt the slightest flicker of interest in what I was seeing, the picture disappeared.

Exasperated, I told Eric, 'I can't get it.'

'Patience,' he said. 'It will take many nights.'

Over the next weeks, I kept trying to relax and drift. Each time, I saw the same stones. The same stones, over and over. Then one night, the stones opened onto a cobbled street. I could see a man pushing a cart. He was wearing old-fashioned clothes. I felt excited. I lost the image.

I had thought the pebbles were going to be on a beach, but this was much more interesting. Be calm, I told myself, be relaxed and open. I looked again and saw the man was wearing clogs.

Along the street I saw wooden buildings and skinny chickens. There was a woman in a long drab-coloured dress. I kept losing the picture, but I went back to it again and again, holding it in my mind for a few minutes at a time.

'What was that about?' I asked Eric afterwards.

'You're learning to see,' he told me, 'by learning how to look.'

I had spent weeks working towards seeing that scene and I had expected specific information to come from it. But it was an obscure scene that meant nothing to me. I felt cheated.

I never saw the pebbles or the street again, but a few days later I saw yellow sand. I forced myself to just sit back inside and look at the picture. It stretched in length and, gradually, I could see water on the edge of the sand – and palm trees. I had never been out of England and I had never seen a beach like it. I did not know whether it was a real place or not; all I knew was that I had never seen anything so beautiful.

I looked to my right and there was a rock pool. I could hear water running over the rocks. The picture was so clear; it was more real than watching a movie. It was as if I had been taken there; I was spellbound.

After a few minutes, the picture faded. I realized then that I didn't have to see only bad things, like the plane crash; I could experience lovely things too.

Another night, not long after, the bed shook so vigorously that Andy woke up.

'The bloody bed's shaking,' he said.

'You can feel it?'

'Of course I can bloody feel it.'

'I told you,' I said, relieved. 'The bed's been shaking for weeks.'

'Well, stop it,' Andy said.

'Pack it in,' I said. I hoped my voice sounded more confident than I felt.

The shaking stopped.

A few nights later, I woke and I could hear Tanya making a noise. I dragged myself out of bed and went to her. Through her doorway, I could see her duvet on the floor and her teddy bear wedged in by her head. She was fast asleep.

I heard Andy call out for me, turned back to the bedroom and saw myself lying next to him. Instantly, I was back in our bed, looking up at the ceiling. It was as if I had never left.

Heart pounding, I started to get out of the bed. I swung my legs over the side and saw my body was still lying there. As soon as I was aware of this, I was back in my body again. The third time, I wriggled my fingers and brought my arm up slowly. Through the light shining from the hall into the bedroom, I saw my arm and realized I could see straight through it. It consisted of a pinky-red light filled with layers and layers of tiny darts of white electricity, all moving quickly.

Sweat pouring down the sides of my face, I sat up and then I really did climb out of bed. Walking to the toilet to wash my face, I passed Tanya's room and looked in – it was exactly as I had seen it – even her duvet was in a tangle on the floor. I couldn't have known that unless I'd been there.

I was up all night, considering the implications of what had happened. My spirit body had left my physical body, so they *had* to be two different things. That meant when the body died, the spirit didn't necessarily die.

I recalled that, as I walked to Tanya's room in my spirit body, I had all the same emotions and thoughts as I had in my physical body. That meant that spirits were stuck with exactly the same emotions. It rocked my atheist beliefs to the core.

I was queuing at the checkout in Tesco's. As I got closer to the woman in front of me, I felt as if my body was moving through quicksand. I was overcome by gloom. I stepped back from her and the feeling lifted.

Out on the street, I walked past a group of men. One of them was angry and, when I came within a foot of him, it was like being hit by a bolt of electricity.

On the way home, I said aloud, 'Why did that woman feel weird in the supermarket?'

'You were picking up her energy,' Eric said.

'But it felt heavy and uncomfortable,' I told him. 'And what about the guy in the street?'

'You noticed the difference?'

'Of course I did.'

'He was feeling a different emotion, so you felt a different energy.'

After that, I experimented with walking close to people to see what I could pick up. When my aura brushed against someone else's, I would get their predominant emotion. It was delicious to be near someone who was happy. I'd get a tingle of excitement, like champagne bubbles popping.

I was in the Light Bite Café in Sheerness, waiting to pick up Tanya from play school. I was bored and I found myself staring at a woman a few tables away. Recently, I had begun to realize that if I slightly unfocused my eyes, I could see white light around people – as I had with the healer at the Spiritualist Church.

I was sitting there, daydreaming and looking at the light around the woman, when a series of pictures suddenly flashed in my head. I saw her crying, and a man shouting at her. Then I saw her walk away from him and slam a door. The pictures were so vivid, I knew she had just had a row with her partner.

It was a shock. I felt suddenly as if I was prying. I got out of the café quickly and started heading for the playschool. I took the route along the beach so that I could talk to Eric. As soon as I was out of sight of anyone else, I called him.

'Eric.'

'Yes.'

'What happened? What was that? I was looking at a woman and I saw pictures. Was I reading her mind?'

'No, you were seeing what caused the emotion she was feeling.'

This was a whole new development.

'Can I do this with anybody?'

'You have the ability to see anyone's emotions.'

I felt as if I had suddenly been given x-ray glasses. I was excited and expectant; impatient to find out what I could do next. Over the next weeks, I started dipping into people. I felt a bit like Superman must have felt when he realized he could see through walls. My sixth sense was starting to develop and my fear was ebbing away.

My friend Janet was one of the first people I told about my burgeoning gift. I had imagined she would be cynical but, to my surprise, she was curious and actually encouraged me to carry on.

A few nights later I was in a pub with her, scanning to see if I could go into anyone. There were a couple of lads at the bar and I locked eyes with one of them, then looked away. Images started to come very quickly. I saw a blonde girl in stockings and suspenders, lying on a bed and looking up seductively. Although he was just standing there, talking to his mate, I could feel him being aroused by the picture in his head. I was shocked.

'Oh my god,' I said to Janet. 'All that bloke's got on his mind is sex.'

I told her what I had done.

'It was like being a bloke for a few minutes,' I said. 'I really saw it from a male point of view.'

'That'll teach you to be nosy,' Janet said.

Curiosity was getting the better of me. And it was highly educational. Through getting flash images and feeling strangers' emotions – albeit very briefly – I truly experienced other people's views of the world.

I began to realize that people live in emotional spaces; everyone exists in how they feel emotionally right now. They don't consider how they felt yesterday or how they might feel tomorrow; all they are aware of is their immediate all-consuming feeling.

I also realized that everyone lives in their own head, looking out at the world and judging it in relation to themselves. There could be 20 people at a party and they would all be having different experiences of the same party. Yet no one has the sense that what they are feeling is just a different viewpoint, a different perspective.

The flashes of insight into the lives of strangers fascinated me, but I had no way of knowing if what I was seeing was true.

'You ought to practise,' Janet said one morning.

'Yes,' I said. 'I suppose so.'

'Try it on me,' she said. 'See what happens.'

We were sitting opposite each other at her kitchen table. Our kids were at school.

'Okay,' I said nervously.

I looked above her head, trying to see her aura. I could see a faint white outline. I grinned at her and, as she smiled back, we made eye contact. As I looked back up to her aura, I took the memory of her eyes with me. All I could see in my mind were her eyes; they seemed to get closer and closer, as if I was going into them. Then I looked at her.

'I know how you feel,' I said. 'You've got an ache in your side and you've got a bit of a sore throat.'

Janet nodded.

'Oh, and you need to undo your jeans,' I said. 'They're too tight.'

Janet was laughing.

'Am I right? Is that right?'

'Yes, you're totally right, carry on,' she said. 'See if you can get anything else.'

'I see a mug breaking on the kitchen floor,' I said.

'Luke dropped a mug this morning.'

'Really?' I was feeling excited. 'Was it by the sink?'

'Yes,' Janet said. 'He meant to put it in the sink but he missed and dropped it on the floor.'

I had seen it. I could hardly believe it. Then another image came.

'I can see the back wheel of a pushchair.'

'I'm having trouble with the wheel,' Janet said. 'I can't get the brake off.'

I stopped and looked at her. I was amazed and excited but also a little confused. Everything I'd seen was trivial; I hoped that soon I would get something big.

I couldn't wait to try again, so I told my friend Bernadette.

'I think I'm turning psychic.'

I did not mention Eric; I knew that would be too weird for anyone but Mum.

'I think I've got the ability to see things about people.'

'Have a go with me, then,' Bernadette said.

I had convinced myself the people close to me would think the whole thing was crazy. I was surprised that, like Janet, Bernadette was so open. From my experience with Janet, I realized that really looking into someone's eyes was the best contact I could make. The fact that I was being given permission to go in made it even easier.

Bernadette always gave the impression that she and her husband had the perfect marriage but now, as I went into her, I felt irritation, frustration and loneliness. She had all these negative feelings about her husband but she was keeping them hidden away. I was inexperienced; I blurted it out.

'You didn't tell me you were feeling like that about Michael.'

Bernadette looked at me.

'What do you mean?'

'You feel you're doing three times as much as he is.'

Tears welled up in her eyes.

'It's true,' she said.

Then she opened up and began to tell me all about it. We got closer that day. It was an honour. I had the ability to know people on a deeper level than I had ever imagined I could.

8

'Hurry up,' I shouted up the stairs to Shane. 'Come down and have your breakfast.'

It was 8.30 in the morning; the kids were due at school in 20 minutes. Andy was still in bed.

'Shut the fuck up,' he yelled.

He was still ill and had now been off work for a year. Usually I did everything I could to keep the peace, but this morning I was running late and I was tense. My tone was sarcastic.

'Sorry for waking you,' I shouted back.

I heard a bang from the bedroom then Andy running downstairs. He backed me into the dining room. He was red in the face.

'You always have to be mouthing off,' he shouted. 'You can't shut up.'

As he came towards me, I moved away until my back was pressed against the wall.

'I'm running late,' I said. 'I'm just trying to hurry the kids up.'

I was trying to appease him, but it was too late. Andy drew back his fist and punched me on the mouth. It was the first time he'd hit me. He stood there in shock; he did not move. I went to the airing cupboard on the other side of the room and grabbed a towel. I put the towel over my face; instantly my hand was wet – the towel was soaked with blood.

Andy had not moved; he was just standing there, still facing the wall. The telephone was on a small table at the bottom of the stairs. I dialled 999 and asked for an ambulance.

'What happened?' a woman asked me.

'I've fallen down the stairs,' I said, concocting a story as I spoke. 'I smashed my face on the table.'

Andy was still motionless. He turned round and I could see he was in shock.

'Take Shane to school and Tanya to playschool,' I directed. 'And don't forget, Tanya comes out at 11.30.'

Andy didn't answer; he just kept looking at me.

The ambulance arrived; the police came too.

'He's hit you, hasn't he?' the police officer said.

'No,' I said. 'I've fallen down the stairs.'

'We can take him away now, it will be all right.'

'No,' I said. 'I fell down the stairs.'

'Do you want us to take the children?'

'No,' I said. 'No.'

'She's losing too much blood,' the ambulance man said. 'We've got to get her to hospital.'

The yellow towel was soaked red and blood was running down my neck, down my arm. My face was distorted. I could not seem to move my mouth.

'Can you sort the kids out?' I mumbled through the towel. Andy nodded.

In the ambulance, the nurse examined my face.

'You could have a fractured jaw there, love,' he said.

At the hospital, I lay on a trolley with a blanket over me. My heart was thudding. Would the bleeding ever stop?

'Eric,' I called to him in my head. 'Eric, Eric.'

Then I heard him.

'It's okay,' he said. 'It's not as bad as you think. Close your eyes.'

I shut my eyes and a wonderful sense of peace crept over me. It was still with me when I was transferred by ambulance to a specialist hospital nearby.

'Three teeth have come out and a fourth is hanging,' the doctor told me.

The teeth had to be removed from where they had lodged: one in the roof of my mouth, another in my cheek. The man who did this to me came to collect me from the hospital later that day. He was contrite.

'I didn't know I'd hit you so hard.'

Andy was desperate for me to come back; he even promised to see a psychiatrist. I kept picturing him the way he was after he punched me – standing there, staring at the wall. Even when the police turned up, he had not moved, had not said a word. He was shocked by what he'd done and was genuinely distressed. I could not hate him – I felt sorry for him.

Andy bought a blender. For the first time since we married, he cooked – meat, mashed potatoes and gravy. He blended a portion for me and I ate it like baby food. He never asked me to lie – if he had, it might have been easier to be angry with him. As it was, I wanted to protect him – him and me.

Mum came over and, for a long time, she just looked at me. I knew that she knew.

'I fell down the stairs,' I told her. I refined my story, to make it more plausible. 'I was walking down the stairs with a glass in one hand and the clock in the other and I caught my foot on my dressing gown and fell. I landed with my face on the table.'

I hated lying to Mum but I couldn't bear to tell her the truth.

'How do you feel now?' she asked me.

I knew she was really asking me if I wanted to talk about it, but if I discussed it I'd have to make decisions I wasn't ready to make.

'I'm fine,' I said.

Later that night, when Andy was asleep, I lay beside him and cried. My husband had hurt me – did that mean I had to think about leaving him? I knew I ought to act and make changes, but it all felt too big.

My face was a constant reminder to Andy of what he had done. He used to sit in the chair with his head in his hands.

'I can't believe I did that to you,' he said.

He felt bad about not being able to work, that he couldn't afford to buy the children new clothes and shoes. I worked at making him feel better.

'We've got a roof over our heads,' I said. 'Things could be worse.'

He began cooking meals and taking the children to school. He even took me away for a few days to Sidmouth in Devon. It was our first holiday – it could have been the honeymoon we never had. But Andy was depressed and, with my mouth stitched and swollen, I felt too ugly and self-conscious to speak to anyone. Up to that point, I had kept trying at the relationship; I thought it might spark back up. But in Sidmouth I realized: it was all too late.

I had to wait for the swelling to go down before the dentist could make impressions for dentures. I was embarrassed to go out. The good thing about being grounded for four months was that family and friends visited all the time and I could experiment with my new seeing skills.

One evening, I was sitting around with a few friends and a bottle of wine, playing with what I could see, when I heard Eric's voice.

'It's not a party trick.'

My relationship with Eric was not only inner – it was also about communicating with people on a deep level. The way that I'd been given to do this was to tune into the bigger picture of someone's life. It enabled me to see beyond the obvious.

Word got around. Family told friends and friends told their families. It was during this period that people began seeking me out. I started doing readings on a regular basis. Initially, when sitting with someone, I would get up to five minutes of information, but this gradually went up to 20 minutes and then half an hour, but I was still my old flippant self.

Sometimes when I was throwing out one-liners, I would hear Eric say, 'You're not feeling them deeply enough,' or 'Don't judge them,' or 'Look again, you're not looking properly. You are missing the obvious.'

He was teaching me how to look and how to read what I was seeing. Some people might say that Eric was an escape, but he took me closer to myself. When I sat and opened up to this being who was with me, I felt calm and plugged into an energy which helped me put life into perspective.

Increasingly, I stopped feeling that I had a party trick to show off. I was experiencing people's emotions and stepping into the inner sanctum of their lives. It felt an honour, a privilege.

When I saw a picture, there was a huge temptation to add to it with my imagination. The person sitting with me would be so excited by what I was seeing and I was so afraid I wasn't giving enough, that I would feel compelled to add to the picture. I tried to take it to what I thought was its logical conclusion. This led to mistakes.

I deciphered things wrongly sometimes, too. One time I saw lights around a friend's stomach and said, 'It looks like you're going to be pregnant.' In fact, she had problems with her period.

I would talk to Eric afterwards and ask, 'Why did I get it wrong?'

His answer was always the same, 'Because you jumped to the conclusion that seemed obvious to you.'

It took time for me to have the confidence to just say what I saw, however incomplete or lame it seemed to be. Eric was deconditioning me, encouraging me to think new thoughts, not to rely on old assumptions. The process of tuning in brought me to a quiet sense of myself, but it took time. And practice. It was a training to keep my heart open.

I needed compassion to connect with the person in front of me and I needed enough detachment to see their story without being overwhelmed. Compassion and detachment – it was a balance and both states were essential. The more I practised, the more I could see.

Every reading was different and I never knew what I was going to see. When I looked in Tom's eyes, I saw a dead woman lying on the ground; another woman with her child face down in the dust. I sensed heat. I was filled with an emotion I couldn't explain.

'I can see a hot, dusty, African village with dead women and children piled together, covered with flies,' I said.

I was shaking and felt on the verge of tears.

'I see an open-topped jeep with men sitting inside. All along the road, there are spikes in the earth and on top of each spike is a white man's head.' I stopped. 'I don't know what I'm talking about.'

Tom was very pale.

'No one – not even my wife – knows about that,' he said. And then he told me, 'After leaving the army, I worked for a couple of years as a mercenary. It was in Angola. We lost the other team and what you saw is what we saw when we found them. I stopped being a mercenary after that,' he said. 'I have never spoken about it.'

'Was it the worst thing that ever happened to you?'

'Yes.'

'That's why I picked it up,' I said. 'That's why it was so strong.'

Shane wasn't sleeping; he was impatient and frustrated. I asked Eric why.

'He's got hearing problems,' he said.

'But he passed his pre-school hearing test.'

'He can't hear properly,' Eric said again.

For a five-year-old, Shane's speech wasn't good; he couldn't communicate as fluently and as quickly as he wanted to. I thought about the way Shane liked to put his hands on my cheeks and turn my face towards him. I always thought he did it for attention, but now I wondered if maybe Eric was right. Maybe Shane wanted to see my mouth when I spoke.

The next time I took Shane for his heart check, I asked the doctor to test his hearing.

'Pass me the blue brick, Shane,' she said.

He did as she instructed. Then she covered her mouth with her hand.

'Pass me the yellow brick, Shane,' she said.

He just looked at her, without moving. I was amazed.

'He's learned to lip read,' the doctor informed me. 'That's how he passed his hearing test.'

The doctor arranged for Shane to have an ear operation and, after that, his speech improved.

By this time, word had got around and more and more people were turning up at the house. I did a reading for Mum's friend and found myself asking for her ring. I held it and saw a girl standing by water. She was having a picnic with a man. When I told her, the woman's face relaxed into a smile.

'That was when my husband proposed. That's when he gave me that ring,' she said.

Another time, I saw the blurred outline of a man in a biker's jacket standing beside the woman I was talking to. I could see the leather tassels on his sleeves; he had a crash helmet in his hands. As I looked at him, I had a flash in my head of a motorbike crashing into a lorry.

'A close friend of mine was killed in a motorbike crash,' the woman told me.

She was moved by her love for her friend. The love was there even after death.

One day I was sitting with Pete and I heard Eric say, 'Look at his eyes.'

It was as if I was inside Pete, looking out, rather than outside, looking in. I could feel his aches and pains.

'There is a tall black man standing behind you,' I told Pete. 'His name is Ray.'

Later, Eric told me that Ray was Pete's guide.

'We all have guides,' he told me. 'But not everyone hears them.'

People started wanting to be near me to see if I could pick things up. I was everyone's pet curiosity. They wanted help – advice and reassurance – and I didn't have the heart to say no. The telephone rang constantly.

Andy didn't like this at all. His remorse about what he'd done was beginning to wear thin, and he was angry again, about a lot of things. He hated it when friends and strangers turned up at our house.

My friend Bernadette came up with a solution.

'Why don't you start charging?' she said. 'Then you could pay for a babysitter.'

That night I spoke to Eric.

'Can I charge?' I asked.

'If that enables people to ask you and enables you to do it,' he answered. 'How can that be bad?'

'What if I give a lousy reading?'

Eric's advice was practical. 'Don't take the money until after the reading,' he said. 'If you're not happy, don't take the money.'

'But what about giving value for money?'

'It's not what you say, it's the feeling behind it,' Eric said. 'Start with mother love. Think of how a mother loves a child.'

Mother love is totally without judgement, totally impartial. Pure mother love is not self-serving. A mother does what's best for the child, not what's best for her. It felt like a very pure energy. Unconditional love.

I asked Eric how I could see something more than random images.

'Use visualization,' Eric told me. 'Look for what you want to know.'

Up until that point, I thought I could only get information that appeared to me. I had not realized I could be focused about what I saw.

'Use a visual image connected with the subject you want to look at,' Eric said. 'Then let it run.'

For the next weeks, still not charging, I practised. I knew people were always keen to know about their finances, so I experimented picturing a stack of coins beside my friends. Nothing happened.

I had to hone the image, find my own pictorial language. I visualized a grid with months down one side and pound signs along the bottom. Then I would sit back inside myself and see what happened. I'd see a line forming in peaks and troughs – a graph of someone's fortunes.

For relationships, I experimented putting hearts above people's heads. That didn't work. So I tried visualizing Cupid and also drew a blank. Gradually, I developed a technique where I pictured the person in an empty room and put a shadowy outline beside them. Then I sat back and waited to see who would fill it.

9

After a few weeks, I felt ready. Bernadette had a friend who was happy to pay. I telephoned a few clairvoyants to see what they were charging – and then decided to halve it and ask for £5.

Ten o'clock on Monday, I set off for Bernadette's house to meet my first fee-paying client. Nervous, I dressed up in a skirt and blouse, rather than my usual jeans and a sweatshirt.

Bernadette introduced us. The woman looked well-groomed and wealthy. She was wearing a suit and a Rolex watch. She was not the type of person I was used to reading for at all.

Bernadette showed us into the lounge. 'I'll stay in the kitchen and finish the ironing,' she said.

We sat opposite each other at the dining-room table. I needed to be relaxed to see images, but my heart was pounding. I was convinced I was going to disappoint us both.

'I'm just going to close my eyes to relax and get ready to see what I can see,' I said.

I closed my eyes, but instead of attempting a relaxation exercise, I called for Eric.

'Eric.'

'Yes.'

'Why am I doing this? Nothing is going to happen.'

'It doesn't matter if you see anything or not,' Eric said, 'as long as you try.'

I opened my eyes and looked at the woman's eyes for the first time. Then I looked away and went into the image of her eyes exactly as I did with my friends. What I saw confounded all my expectations. On the surface, she looked in control of her life – she looked like all I aspired to be – but underneath she was a mess of self-doubt and worry.

'You're feeling insecure,' I told her. 'You worry too much about the little things. You need to learn to relax.'

She nodded, but did not say anything. A picture floated into my mind: I saw a house surrounded by fields, which I described to her. Then I saw a dovecote with doves flying around it. I wanted to tell her what I was seeing but, as I opened my mouth to speak, I lost my confidence.

'I can see a lot of birds around your house,' I said hesitantly.

I watched her face, waiting for her to say, 'That's rubbish.'

'Actually,' she said, 'I've got a dovecote.'

A *dovecote*. In that moment, I decided to say exactly what I saw. I used the techniques I had been honing and told her about her children and her work.

Then I visualized the relationship room, put her inside it and placed a shadow next to her. The shadow moved to the other side of the room; I knew then that she was with someone but they were not connecting properly. There was a big gap between them.

Being a reader is like being a detective; the images are clues. Then you have to sit with them, unravel their meaning. I waited, watching the picture. Gradually, the outline of the man took small steps back towards her.

'You're in a relationship but you're living two separate lives.'

She nodded.

'He will come back to you,' I said. 'There's nothing for you to do. He will do it. It looks like it will take months.'

She started to cry.

'I think my husband is having an affair,' she said. 'Is he?'

The images in my head were clear, but I did not have the confidence to tell her what I saw; if I was wrong about the affair, the implications were enormous. My instincts told me that she knew the answer. What she really wanted to know was whether he was going to leave her.

'Be patient. In a few months, you will be back together,' I said. 'Everything is going to be all right.'

She paid me £5. That night I took the kids to the Wimpy and we all had burgers and chips.

'I think I can charge for my readings,' I told Andy the next morning.

'I don't mind as long as I don't have to look after the kids,' he said.

I began to see clients in the kitchen in the mornings when the children were at school. Everyone came through word of mouth and the more readings I did the better I became at communicating what I saw.

In the beginning, I was blunt – just blurting out what I was seeing, before rushing onto the next thing. Now I began to take time to talk in more depth about the meaning of what I was seeing.

I started doing readings in the evenings, too. Sometimes the kids would get out of bed and call for me and I had to interrupt a reading to sort them out. I might be stressed, but I learnt that whatever the domestic chaos, I always finished a reading feeling relaxed and calm. I was left with a feeling of strength that lasted for hours.

At night in bed, I still 'sat back' inside myself, watching the images that came. One night, I felt I was in the air, flying above trees. I was startled and lost it. It's okay, I told myself, you're not really flying. It's only a picture. I refocused, relaxed. I was about 30 feet above a huge canopy of trees in a rainforest, so dense it was hard to see between the leaves.

I saw a flock of brightly-coloured birds and a wide, slow-moving river. The picture was so strange and so wondrous, it was hard to remain impassive. But every time I got excited, I lost the picture. I had to control my emotions in order to see it again.

'Eric.'

'Yes.'

'Did I go there? Have I seen an actual forest?'

'What do you believe?'

I felt irritable. 'I wouldn't be asking you if I knew what it was.'

'I'm not going to answer all the questions for you,' Eric said.

The next time I 'flew', it was over mountains. Again I was seeing things I had never seen before and yet they seemed so real. I saw ravines and trees dusted with snow like icing sugar. I saw a herd of animals that looked like antelopes and a clear crisp-looking lake.

The air felt clean and light. I knew it was cold, but I did not feel chilled. I was in awe. The feeling of flying was fantastic – I felt so free. It was like swimming without water. The only thing that stopped me was my own reactions. Then I had to calm down and go back in.

One night, I saw a reef and tiny shoals of amazingly vivid fish. I had never seen colours like it. I realized I was under water and, even though it was not necessary, I held my breath.

It was like having a magical picture book that I could dip into. Playtime. It was total pleasure.

One night, I had some precious time alone and I was talking with Eric in the front room, when I asked him, 'Have you been on Earth? Have you been alive?'

'Of course,' he answered.

'When?'

'A long time ago.'

I had the feeling that he was under guidelines or rules; that he was telling me as much as he was allowed.

'Where did you live?' I asked him.

'I'll show you,' he said.

I started floating, waiting for him to show me pictures. I saw my feet; I was standing on bracken and bits of nettle. I sat, waiting for the picture to change then I heard Eric's voice.

'Well, walk then,' he said.

His tone was gentle but frustrated. I took a couple of steps.

'Bring your senses with you,' Eric instructed. 'Hear it, smell it, see it. You are here.'

I concentrated, using every bit of my imagination to forget I was in the chair in my front room. I looked up from my feet and saw a path between trees. Eric was walking in front of me. I could hear twigs breaking underfoot and rustling in the undergrowth. I smelt damp earth, grass and wood smoke.

I followed Eric down a slope and saw a clearing. Eric was sitting by the fire, on the stump of an old tree. He looked up and motioned me towards a large mossy log on the other side of the fire.

I could feel the texture of the bark through my clothes. I ran a hand over the tree, it was soft and crumbly. Through a gap in the trees, I could see a narrow round stone building.

Every time I'd 'travelled', I'd felt I was an observer; unheard and unseen by anything around me. I could view but I was not a part of it. This time, however, I knew I was in the image. I could smell it, touch it, hear it. The animals in the undergrowth knew I was there.

I looked at Eric and he half smiled at me. He did not seem to be visiting; this place was a part of him, he was comfortable and at home here. I'm where he is, I thought, I'm in his space. I felt excited and enthralled. The picture started to dissolve. I could feel my hands on the arm of the chair. I was back in my living room.

I had stepped into another world. It felt magical. After a few moments, I knew Eric was back in the room with me.

'Is that where you lived?' I asked. 'Is it still there?'

'Not as it was.'

'Did we go to a real place,' I asked him, 'or a memory?'

His answer was open-ended.

'For me,' he said, 'it is real.'

Up until that point, he'd always come to my space, now I'd been to his place. I was to return there again and again.

One evening, a woman came to see me; I knew instantly that she was lonely. I couldn't picture her in the relationship room; instead, I saw her standing outside the Post Office in Sheerness.

'I see you bumping into a man wearing a tweed jacket with leather patches on his elbows. He is saying, "Hello, my name's Bob," and you are smiling at each other. It will happen in the next week or two,' I said.

After she had left, I thought about what I'd said – leather patches, Bob. How could I be so specific? I was convinced I had got it wrong.

The woman rang me three weeks later.

'Mia,' she said. 'It's just as you described. I was in Sheerness Post Office when a guy bumped into me. He had a tweed jacket on, with corduroy patches on the elbows. He said sorry and we got talking. We've been on two dates and he's really nice,' she said. 'His name is Bill.'

I put the phone down and sat in stunned silence. I'd got a few things wrong – his name was Bill rather than Bob and the patches were corduroy not leather – but apart from those tiny details, it had happened as I'd seen. I was amazed at the powers that enabled me to see ahead of time.

'Trust your instinct,' Eric always said. I vowed to have more faith. 'See it and say it,' as Eric said.

The hard part was trusting myself. I started practising, saying things exactly as I saw them. A woman came to see me because she was worried about her husband. In the relationship room, I saw another woman. I started to describe her, 'She has got straight dark hair and dark eyes; she is wearing a blue dress.'

I heard a name as a whisper.

'Karen or Sharon,' I said.

'That would be Sharon,' the woman said.

'You know he's having an affair, don't you?'

'I wasn't sure,' the woman replied, 'that's why I came to see you.'

'The worst thing is,' I said, 'she's meant to be your friend.'

The woman started to cry.

'A storm is coming, but in three months time, you'll feel better,' I assured her.

An hour after she left, there was a banging on the front door. Andy was out. I went to see who it was.

'Who the fuck do you think you are?' the man on the doorstep yelled at me. 'Do you have any idea the sort of damage lies like yours can do?'

'It's not a lie. You're having an affair. Why are you shouting at me?'

I shut the door. Bloody men, I thought. I still felt I had done the right thing in telling the woman what I saw.

'Are we playing God now?' Eric's voice was in my head.

'I only told the truth,' I said.

'There are many ways of telling the truth,' Eric said.

I realized I had not looked closely enough: did the woman really want to know about his affair? Could she cope with the information? I had jumped in with both feet and said what I saw. I realized that it was not right and I regretted it.

It was a lesson. Up until that point, it had all been about how much I could receive. Now I realized that was only the beginning. A good psychic needs wisdom in the telling of information. You have to care for the person; you get the story, but the way you tell it needs awareness. You have to care about a person's life in the long term. A good psychic helps people through crisis points in their life – helping them to see the bigger picture. Everything is always changing – hope follows despair.

I needed to step aside and not put myself on a pedestal. If vanity got in the way, it blurred the picture. The people who came to see me were not there for me to prove how clever I was, they were there to get help.

A woman rang and asked if I could do a party booking.

'Five of us want a reading,' she said.

Andy would go berserk with all those people in the house.

'You can do it at my house,' she said.

Walking up the driveway to the big detached bungalow in Leysdown, I felt intimidated. A middle-aged woman answered the door; she was wearing lots of gold jewellery. When she saw me, she looked surprised. She had been expecting a manic old lady with a blue rinse, not a girl in jeans who was young enough to be her daughter.

She took me into the lounge to meet the other women. They looked similar: bright clothes, gold jewellery and bleached permed hair. The disappointment in the room was palpable; they had picked the wrong psychic.

I stood there in my jeans, black rollneck jumper and boots, clutching a battered packet of cigarettes. I wanted to go home. If I wasn't any good, I wouldn't charge them.

I sat opposite the first woman, my heart thumping and my hands sweating. How was I going to open up and do a reading? I looked into her eyes and, instantly, I knew she was the same as me – as everyone. No matter what the attitude on the outside, we are all suffering human beings who want to be happy.

When I arrived, they treated me like a child; when I left they were treating me as a mother. My work broke down all barriers. This was my first experience of the way clairvoyance can cut through the divisions between people. It was yet another reminder not to worry about what people thought of me. The important thing was to try to help them – to go to the crux of their lives and love them, warts and all.

Around this time, a 21-year-old man came for a reading. I could see straightaway that he was in darkness. I was only five years older than him but instantly I felt as if he was my kid brother. He was visibly stressed and shaking slightly, so I tried to make him feel relaxed.

I started with a health scan, imagining a beam of light travelling through his body. He was young and healthy-looking: I did not expect it to take long. But when I got to his diaphragm, I saw that something was massively out of balance. I scanned three times to make sure I could understand what I was seeing. Then I got a clear image of a needle and I saw him injecting himself.

This was my first contact with someone who used drugs. I was shocked. I looked into his eyes again and I saw terrible pain. A feeling of love came over me. I wanted to cuddle and protect him; I wanted to make it all right.

'I can see needles and toxins going into your body,' I said. 'I can also see your depression and despair which means you can't handle this. You are not in control.'

He broke down, his body racked with sobs. I gave him a box of tissues and let him cry it out.

'I'm never going to be able to stop,' he said.

I saw a picture of a hangman's noose around his neck.

'You're considering killing yourself,' I said.

'No, I'm not considering it,' he said. 'I'm going to do it.'

I couldn't let him out of my house, I knew it, not until we sorted this out. The reading was meant to last 45 minutes – I had the ironing to do and I had to make the kids' packed lunches – but every reading I had ever given had been working towards this moment. The man in front of me was going to kill himself. It was the heaviest reading I had done.

I broke off from the reading and made us both a cup of coffee. All the time feverishly thinking how I could help him.

'I came to ask you something,' he told me as we drank our coffee. 'I want to know what happens to people who kill themselves. Where do they go? What happens to their spirits?'

'If you cop out and take your own life,' I told him, 'it's like getting expelled from school. When you get home to your Mum and Dad they'll send you to another one.'

Mother love – at that moment, I knew what it was to care deeply for a stranger. I felt mother love and the words came out. I told him that when I was a teenager, I didn't believe in God or anything spiritual. I then detailed how I met Eric and how he taught me that life is a school.

'You are having the hardest lesson early in life,' I said. 'In my experience, nobody moves on from a bleak situation until they hit rock bottom. Then there's only one way to go. That's where you are now.'

'But I've tried to change,' he said. Tears were rolling down his face. 'I've tried to stop and I go for a little while, then I take it again.'

'Six months ago, you didn't even want to stop taking it,' I reminded him. 'Can't you see the massive steps you've taken? You're waking up. The pain means you care. This is the first step out of the pit.'

We spent two hours talking. At the end of it, I felt as if I had done a 100-yard dash with a fragile egg – and arrived at the finishing line with it, unbroken. I handed the egg to him, knowing it was going to be okay. His life was going to be a roller-coaster for a while, but he was going to come through. I rarely cuddle people, but I gave him a quick hug at the door.

'Your despair is the tool you can use to move on,' I told

him. 'Remember the pain you feel now. In years to come, you will use it to help others.'

'Do you think so?'

'I know so.'

He kept in touch and went on to take a sociology degree and became a social worker. At the time, I felt it was the most useful reading I had done. I was there at the right time and I made a difference.

'Oh Eric,' I said.

I knew he was around. He knew what had happened.

'Well done,' Eric said.

Shortly after this, I was asked to help get rid of a ghost for some friends of Pete's. For the past few months they had been experiencing strange goings-on in their house.

'Things keep being moved,' Vicki told me on the telephone. 'Lights are turned off and doors close. Last night we put a cheesecake on top of the gas fire to defrost while we were watching TV. We both saw it come off the top of the fire and slowly move to the floor. It freaked the hell out of us.'

'I can't promise anything,' I said, 'but I'll come round and see if there's anything I can do.'

As soon as I put the phone down, I called Eric.

'What do you do with a ghost?' I asked him. 'Can we get rid of one?'

As usual, there were no guarantees from Eric.

'Go round and have a look,' he said. 'See what you can see.'

That night, when the children were in bed, I went to Vicki and Mark's. It was dark; walking up to the house I felt like something out of *The Exorcist*. I also felt a fraud. I didn't have a clue what I was going to do if I actually saw a ghost.

In the front room, Vicki said, 'We're so glad you've come, we've been so worried.'

Oh God, I thought, she really thinks I'm going to be able to sort this out. Vicki started to gabble at me, telling me again about all the weird things that had been going on. As I listened, I started to see a shadowy outline behind the couch she and Mark were sitting on. I felt very calm. I knew the best thing was not to let them know it was there.

Out of the corner of my eye, I watched the shape get stronger and more defined. Eventually I could see an old woman standing there. She was wearing a flowery dress with an apron; she had soft grey hair. Vicki was still talking to me. In my head, I called, 'Eric.'

'It's all right,' he said. 'She's been trying to help.'

The woman was smiling at me sweetly; she was holding her hands together. She used to live here, it was her home.

I turned back to Mark and Vicki. I realized that the old lady turned the lights off after they had left the room. Vicki said cups were moved from the sideboard to the cupboard; the old lady was tidying them away.

'When the cheesecake was moved to the floor,' I asked, 'was it ready to eat?'

'Does that matter?' Mark was incredulous. 'We're talking about a levitating cheesecake and you're asking if it was edible.'

'Humour me,' I said.

'Well, yeah,' he said, 'I suppose it was. We ate it twenty minutes later and it was perfectly okay.'

I started to explain. 'You have the spirit of an old lady in the house. She has been trying to help. She's been putting things away and turning the lights and TV off so you don't waste electricity.'

Behind them, the old lady nodded at me.

'She didn't want you to ruin your cheesecake,' I said. 'The cheesecake had defrosted and if you'd left it on the fire any longer it would have been spoilt.'

'At least it's not a nasty spirit,' Vicki said, 'but can you do something about it? We don't want her in the house.'

'I'll have a go and see what I can do.'

I closed my eyes.

'Eric,' I said in my head, 'what are we going to do?'

His voice was clear.

'Concentrate on the old lady.'

I saw her really clearly; she was glowing. Then I saw a soft, sun-orange glow appear behind her. The glow grew stronger and then turned into an archway. Eric was standing in the archway and he held his hand out to the woman.

The old woman seemed dazed, confused. She looked around the room as if to say: 'This is my home.' Then she looked at Eric again. The woman started to walk towards Eric. She held his hand and they walked through the archway and disappeared.

I was amazed. In awe. In life, she was probably an inconsequential old woman attached to her home, yet the power of tenderness and love coming off Eric towards her was astounding. He was like a father who had found a lost child; as if he recognized she had been lost for a long time. There were no words, but there was a tremendous feeling of 'it's all right now'.

It seemed so far-fetched, I didn't think I could tell anybody what I had seen. But it felt good. I was suffused with a wonderful feeling of knowledge. In that moment I knew, without any doubt, that there was a higher energy – and it had come to collect an old lady.

A doorway had opened to another dimension. Even if they had turned around, I didn't think Mark and Vicki would have seen it.

Vicki broke into my thoughts, 'Are you all right Mia?'

'Yes, I'm fine.'

'Can you get rid of her?'

'Well actually,' I said, 'she's gone. You won't have any more problems with her.'

'How did you do that?'

'That's not something I can discuss,' I said, all the time thinking: 'I haven't got a clue.'

I knew I'd been of help, but I didn't know how. What had I done? As I left the house, I called for Eric but he wasn't around. I said his name a few times in the hours that followed, but he did not reply. Finally, that night, when I was in bed with Andy asleep beside me, I tried once more.

'Eric, Eric, are you there?'

'Yes.'

'Where have you been?'

His answer was evasive.

'I've been busy,' he said.

'Is the old lady okay?'

'She's fine now.'

'What happened? How did that happen? Did you do it? Did I?'

'You are the connection between the dimensions,' Eric said. 'When you hold the connection, then I can work.'

'I don't understand. What do you mean connection between the dimensions?'

'You live in one dimension but you can see in other dimensions; you can see different levels of spirit,' Eric said. 'When you concentrate strongly on the image in another dimension, you make a bridge which I can then work from to take the spirit over.'

'Are we going to do more of this?'

'Most probably,' Eric said.

My head was buzzing. I had so many questions but Eric said, 'That's enough for now.'

I was left with the knowledge that the afterlife is much more complex than humanity thinks it is. There was so much that I – that we – didn't know.

A few weeks later, Vicki told me she had researched the history of her house.

'An old woman did live here,' she told me. 'She had been nursing her husband for a couple of years when she died suddenly of a heart attack.'

I realized then that the old woman had stayed behind because she was worried about her husband; she still thought that she could help.

10

Tanya was bleeding. I looked in the toilet pan; it had blood all around it. I telephoned the emergency doctor.

'It's probably piles,' he assured me. 'Bring her into the surgery in the morning.'

The duty doctor's verdict was the same.

'It will clear itself up,' he said. 'Don't worry.'

But I did worry. I was sure Tanya had something more serious than piles. I tried to do a health scan on her, but the image kept breaking up. I couldn't understand why it wasn't working.

I turned to Eric and asked, 'What is it?'

'Blood.'

'It's obviously blood.' I felt exasperated. 'Where is it coming from?'

'You know where it's coming from.'

I tried again. 'What's causing it?'

'Something's bleeding.'

I wanted a straight answer and he was talking in riddles. I got irritable and stopped talking to him. Tanya was five years old and she was bleeding.

I took her back to the doctor twice more. On the third

visit, he agreed to send her to see a specialist – but the appointment was three weeks away. I felt desperate.

When Mum came round later that day, I said, 'See if you can scan Tanya.'

'Don't be silly,' Mum said, 'I won't be able to do that.'

I knew I was grasping at straws, but I didn't know what else to do.

'There's no harm in trying,' I urged. 'We've got nothing to lose.'

I explained the way I did a health scan.

'Visualize a line of light above Tanya's head and let it come down,' I said.

We were sitting at the kitchen table. Mum closed her eyes.

'I can see the line of light in my mind's eye,' she said.

'Take it down slowly,' I advised.

Then Mum lost the picture completely.

'I'm looking at her bowel,' she said, 'and it's see-through. At the entrance to the bowel there seems to be a lump. The top is broken and bleeding.'

'A lump,' I said, 'you can see a lump?'

'I really don't think it's serious,' Mum said. 'I don't know why, but I feel quite confident about that.'

Tanya went through horrible tests at the hospital; invasive internal exams and endless x-rays – they did not find anything. After two days they were ready to discharge her.

'I think you should look in the bowel,' I told the doctor. 'I believe it's coming from there.'

'It will mean putting her under general anaesthetic,' the

doctor said, 'and I don't think that's necessary.'

'Well I do' – I was trusting all my instincts. 'I think there is something going on in her bowel. I'm not happy for you to discharge her just because you can't find out what it is.'

Reluctantly, the doctor agreed to give Tanya an anaesthetic and examine her internally with a camera.

'You do realize,' he said nastily as they wheeled Tanya into surgery, 'we are putting your daughter under general anaesthetic just to put your mind at rest.'

'That's how you see it,' I said without emotion. I behaved confidently but, in the parents' waiting room, doubt began to take hold. What had I done? What if something happened to Tanya when she was under the anaesthetic? Was I a neurotic mother after all?

Half an hour later, the doctor came to see me.

'We located a large polyp at the entrance to the bowel and managed to cauterize it,' he said. 'The operation has been a complete success.'

A few nights later, I asked Eric.

'Why didn't I see the picture of Tanya's stomach?'

'You could not be unemotional about it,' Eric said.

'How was Mum able to see it?'

'When she looked, she didn't expect to see anything – she was just trying it out – that's how she managed to see the image.'

While all this was going on, things at home were getting worse and worse. Andy was always in a mood. He smashed things – cups and ashtrays mainly, hurling them at the wall. He kicked chairs over and yelled at me. Each time, I thought he was going to punch me. My body cringed; I wanted to be invisible. I was scared of Andy all the time.

It was the Easter holidays; Shane and Tanya were off school. Andy backed me up against the kitchen wall; he was shouting in my face.

'You're a lazy bitch,' he said. 'You do my head in. All you do is cause me stress. You need to sort your fucking act out.'

He drew back his fist and punched the wall by my head. I thought his fist was going to come into my face. I thought he was going to do it to me all over again. I was immobilized with fear. I could not speak or move.

He slowly moved away from me. Still shouting, he grabbed his coat and drove off. After the door slammed, there was stillness. I could hear the children crying upstairs.

'Quick,' I said, trying to sound cheerful. 'Let's get your coats and shoes on, we're going up town.'

Within minutes we were out of the house. I walked straight to the Social Services Department.

'I really need to get away from my husband, I'm frightened of him,' I told the receptionist. 'Can I speak to somebody?'

The children were led away to the play area. I was taken into a side room.

'I've heard about battered wives' hostels,' I told the duty social worker. 'Can you help me get into one?'

'Have you been hit before?'

'Yes.' I felt ashamed.

'Did you press charges?'

'No,' I said. More shame.

150

'Are you frightened he's going to hit you again?'

'Yes.'

The social worker managed to find me a room in a hostel.

'But it's over two hundred miles away,' she said. 'In Bradford.'

I had £3 in my purse.

'How the hell do I get to Bradford?'

'We'll sort you out a travel warrant.'

We took the beach road to the railway station in case Andy saw us. I told the children we were going on a surprise holiday; they were excited about going on the train. I spent the last of my money on fizzy drinks and a packet of biscuits. The journey took four hours.

We arrived in Bradford, a grumpy bundle of exhaustion. I telephoned the hostel for directions and we tramped through the unfamiliar streets. The hostel door was opened by a woman with a chubby face.

'Hello dear,' she said, 'come on in.'

The town house was warm and filled with the noise of children, shouting and playing. I could hear a television. Shane and Tanya stayed really close to me as the woman led us into a big kitchen.

'Do you want to come and play?' a group of kids swarmed around us. Shane ran off immediately, but Tanya clung on. I was given a large steaming mug of tea and, gradually, Tanya went off to explore.

'I haven't got anything with me,' I told the woman at the kitchen table. 'I've got no money. What have I done?'

'Don't worry,' she said gently. 'It's not a problem.'

She offered me a cigarette. I was so grateful.

That night, we all had dinner in the communal kitchen. The women were friendly; the kids played together. I felt safe.

We had been there a week when the social worker suggested I enrol the children in the local primary school. It seemed a big step but they loved it. They were happy. We were all free from fear.

The children had been at the school for two weeks when, one evening, I telephoned Mum.

'Andy has been round to see me,' Mum told me. 'He knows he's been hard to live with. He said he couldn't bear the thought of you and the kids not being there. He said he will do anything to make it better.'

That night I thought of my home, I thought of the children's clothes and toys. I thought of Mum living round the corner. I sat for a while in the day room. I thought about telephoning Andy. Then I picked up the phone.

He answered after the first ring.

'It's me,' I said.

Andy's words came out in a torrent.

'Where are you? Are you all right? Are the kids okay? Please come home. I would never hit you again, I told you that.'

'You scared the bloody life out of me,' I said. 'I can't cope with not knowing what you're going to do next.'

Andy was quiet.

'I understand that,' he said. 'Please come back.'

'If it happens again, I'll go,' I said. 'Next time I won't come back.'

'It won't happen again,' Andy sounded so earnest. 'Just come home.'

A lot of women in refuges do it: make a bid for a life free from fear and beatings and then go back to a violent partner. It was hard for the staff and the women in the refuge; they did not want us to go.

I used the last of my social security to buy train tickets. Andy picked us up at Sheerness station. The kids told him about our 'holiday'. I was very quiet. It was 8 p.m. We bought fish and chips and ate them at the kitchen table before the children went to bed.

Half an hour later, I sat beside Andy on the sofa. The television was on. He spoke without taking his eyes off the screen.

'If you ever take Tanya away from me again, I'll fucking kill you,' he said.

I should never have gone back. I'd been through so much in the last three weeks, only to return to the same situation – only now it was worse. I didn't feel I could return to the social worker and ask to do the whole thing again. I had no money and nowhere to go. I'd had my chance and I had blown it.

Two months later, Andy went crazy again. He started kicking the kitchen chair; he was shouting. The kids were at school. I was terrified. I ran out of the house and locked myself in my old Cortina.

'Get out of the fucking car,' Andy yelled.

I put the keys in the ignition. As I started to drive away, I saw Andy get into his car. As I turned into the road at the end of the street, he rammed his car into the back of mine. I was so scared. I thought he was going to kill me.

I drove to the police station and parked outside. Andy drove past. I sat there for half an hour, wondering whether to go in and get help. I thought there must be a law against ramming a car with somebody in it. But I feared the police would just tell Andy off and it would make things worse.

I drove to Minster and sat on the beach for three hours, waiting to pick the children up from school. I was terrified of Andy. I wanted to leave but if I tried to take Tanya, he would kill me.

I telephoned him.

'You over-reacted again, didn't you?' he said. 'Running off like a headless chicken.'

'Are you all right now?' I always seemed to be asking him the same question, checking whether it was safe to go home.

'Of course I'm bloody all right,' he said.

When we got home, we did not speak about it.

After that, it followed a routine: Andy would lose it and I would get out of the way; a few hours later I'd phone home and go back. He stopped apologizing.

As soon as Andy started shouting, I felt cold fear in my chest. Then I was prepared to do anything to defuse the situation. I pacified and agreed with everything he said and, sometimes, that calmed him.

It was a gradual process, but Andy broke down my confidence and my personality. He decided the food we ate, the furniture we bought, where it was positioned in the house. I was a natural peacemaker – my instinct was for harmony not confrontation. And all the time I lived with a darkness, it was ominous. Something terrible was about to happen.

There were times Andy was pleasant, but I knew it couldn't last. I could never relax around him. Luckily Andy approved of night school – and for me, it meant I could get out of the house. Once a week, I started attending the local college. I studied for 'A' levels – first English, then Maths and Sociology, and I did a course in typing. I passed them all.

But I lost all my power. I had no rights, no voice. Each day was dictated by Andy's mood. I believed I couldn't leave. If I did, he would take Tanya or do something terrible to me. There was no way out.

So many times I asked Eric to help me change the situation. All he ever said was, 'In time'.

I lived in so much fear. Watching television, I would hear Andy's car and I would jump up to look busy. As soon as he walked in the door I asked, 'Can I get you anything?'

I always worried what I was going to cook him, in case he did not like it. Looking back, I see that I didn't help the situation. My peacemaking fed his sense of power. He kept pushing the boundaries, exerting his will over me until I no longer invited friends round or went out without his permission.

I did more and more readings. Going into people's lives took me out of mine. For them, I was the wise one, the person with the answers. But then I had to go back to the turmoil of my own life, which I could not sort out.

Rumours started. Girls I knew would stop me on the street: 'You do know, don't you, what Andy is up to?'

I prayed that he'd find someone else and that he would leave.

One night I received a phone call from an American. She told me she was a writer researching the paranormal.

'I've heard you're a good psychic,' she said. 'Would you be interested in doing some experiments for my book?'

She explained she wanted me to sit in a circle with people, so she could test my psychic abilities. The thought of someone wanting to put me in a book made me feel important. My friend Janet had become increasingly interested in learning about the paranormal and she was keen to test out her own psychic skills, so I invited her along.

Later that week, we met in a flat in Sheerness. The writer was a middle-aged woman in a white suit. She introduced me to two healers, and to a woman in her seventies who, she told me, was a deep-trance medium. There were two other women there: a friend and her secretary.

We sat in a circle. I told everyone, in turn, what I saw. There was a feeling like electricity in the air. The images came easily. It was a joy to work.

We were asked to return the following week.

'I want to see if we can get something physical to manifest,' the writer said. 'See if we can get a spirit to appear or move things in the room.'

That week, I wondered if I would be able to make something happen. I thought the only way to do so would be to send out a call – something I'd never done before. I hoped I would get something that warranted being in the book. I did not want to fail.

We sat in the circle.

The writer said, 'Mia is going to try to make a physical manifestation.'

I closed my eyes and visualized my mind as a ball of light inside my head. Then I visualized it sending beams all over the place. I said in my mind: 'Is there anybody who would like to communicate with me?'

Eric said, 'Stop, don't do this.'

In my ignorance, I thought: 'I can do this but he doesn't want me to.' It gave me confidence to carry on.

Janet said, 'I've got a really strong picture in my mind.'

She was sitting opposite me. I looked at her.

I said, 'Is it the house where you used to live?'

'Yes.'

We were seeing the same picture. We were inside Janet's old house. Then, suddenly, I got a strong picture in my head of a black Rottweiler standing at the top of the stairs. He was slavering and dribbling.

'Oh my God,' Janet said, 'I can see a dog.'

Eric said, 'It's coming.'

There was a warning in his voice; and also resignation. I looked at Janet – everyone else in the room was feeling expectant and excited, but she had felt the horror that was coming – I could see it on her face.

The lamp on the side table went off. The flat was lit now

only by the street lamp. Then I saw it; a black shape behind Janet. It was moving around the back of the circle and, as it arrived behind me, I was filled with a sense of dread – the weight of which I have never experienced. Dread was in my bones, in the pit of my stomach, the cells of my skin. I knew instinctively, this was something bad.

'Eric, Eric.'

He did not answer me.

The black mass was going around the circle for a second time. It was like a million black bees in formation, irregular, shifting shape, changing. The woman on my left started jerking. She was having a fit. I don't know why, but I shoved myself against her and she went quiet.

The woman next to Janet stood up. She wanted to run out of the room.

'Sit down,' I shouted at her. 'Don't break the circle.'

Again, I don't know how I knew to keep it whole. It felt vital to me. We all had to stay there.

'Eric, Eric.'

He did not answer, but I heard a man's voice.

'You know not what you have done.'

The voice was coming from the old lady. I knew I had to look at her, but I also knew I would not like what I saw. Slowly, I turned to look. The old lady's face had a man's face projected onto it, like a movie onto a blank screen. Behind the projection, her mouth was hanging open.

The man's voice said again, 'You know not what you have done.'

I knew the voice belonged to a spirit guide and not the black entity in the room. In my head, I screamed for Eric again.

'It's all right,' he said. 'Concentrate on the cross, concentrate on the cross.'

'What cross?'

'Look for it, you'll see it.'

Suspended in the air, in the centre of the circle, I saw the faint outline of a gold cross.

'I've got it Eric, I'm starting to see it.'

'Just concentrate on it.'

As I focused on the cross, it started to solidify. The entity ran behind me again and the feeling of dread returned – ice cold, all encompassing. I lost the image of the cross. Twice more the entity's proximity chased the image from my head. I had to fight to retain it, to make it solid. The instant I did, there was a flash of light from the cross; it filled the room then went back to the cross.

The lamp came back on and the cross vanished. The trance medium was coming round, blinking her eyes. Two of the women were crying. I was shaking.

'I can't stay here, I've got to get out.' The woman who owned the flat was in tears.

I sat in front of her.

'I know it's scary, but it's gone,' I told her. 'There's nothing left here.'

I turned to the American writer. 'I have to go.'

She stood up.

'That was amazing Mia,' she said. 'Shall we say the same time next week?'

I looked at her in shock. Was she mad?

'No,' I said, 'I'm finished with this.'

Outside on the street, Janet and I lit up cigarettes.

'Did you see it?' I asked her. 'Did you see the black thing?'

'Did I see it?' Janet said. 'I've never been more scared in my life.'

'Did you see the cross?'

'I saw its outline.'

'Eric told me to concentrate on the cross.'

Janet said, 'I kept saying the Lord's Prayer – it was the only thing that came to mind.'

We started walking down the street.

I said, 'I'm never doing anything like that again.'

For three hours, I could not get hold of Eric. I worried he was angry with me. He finally replied when I was in bed.

'Eric.'

'Yes.'

'I'm really, really sorry.'

'You endangered people because of your pride.'

I thought of the woman having a fit and the other women crying.

'I'm sorry.'

Then – I had to ask him, 'Will it come back?'

'You're safe,' Eric assured me. 'It can only come through invitation.'

'I would never have invited that in.' I was indignant.

'Nevertheless,' Eric said, 'you invited it.'

I couldn't get it out of my head: how evil the entity had felt. I knew now, absolute goodness had to exist. I totally believed in the energy of pure goodness because I had seen its opposite.

A few nights later, I asked Eric, 'Why the cross? Did I see a cross because I am Catholic?'

'It's what symbolized goodness for you,' Eric said.

'So someone of a different religion would see a different image?'

'Yes.'

I was afraid to give readings; afraid that when I opened up, I might bring the black energy back. I was experiencing things beyond my imagination. Would I have the courage to confront something like that again?

I felt like someone who thinks she knows how a computer works because she can switch it on and off. Then one day someone takes the back off the computer and shows her the inside. I realized I had only just been scratching the surface. There was so much I didn't know.

'I never could have handled that on my own Eric,' I told him one night. 'If someone had that bad energy in their house, I couldn't cope with it. I have no way of fighting it.'

'Its power is your fear,' Eric said. 'It can't hurt you other than through your fear.'

I remembered how, when the entity came round the back of me, I was totally taken over by fear. It saturated me; it invaded me.

'How can I stop that terror?' I asked Eric. 'It makes you scared, it does something to you.'

'You don't allow it.'

That's how you fight the dark, I thought, you separate from your emotions.

'Was it a bad spirit?'

'It wasn't a spirit,' Eric told me. 'It had never been born. It hadn't walked the earth.'

'Was it from hell?'

'It was from a lower dimension.'

'Is that like hell?' I had to know.

'If that's the way you want to see it,' Eric said.

I thought I was too scared ever to do a reading again. When people rang, I said I was unwell. I could hardly say: 'I've had a fight with an entity from hell so I'm off it at the moment.' But after about six weeks, I began to feel restless. I was not achieving anything, not doing anything worthwhile. Without readings, my life felt meaningless.

One morning, a woman rang for a booking and I said, 'Okay, I can see you today.'

Once I had done the reading, I felt better. I was back in balance.

I was shopping in Sheerness High Street with the children when we bumped into Mick. He looked untidy and thin and spaced-out. I did not know what to say; I had not seen him in seven years.

He looked at Shane.

'Hello.'

Shane looked at his dad. He had no idea who he was.

'Hello,' he said back.

Mick half smiled and carried on walking. I watched him

walk away, slightly staggering.

A few days later, I told Jed that I had seen Mick. I was worried he might want to stir things up for Shane.

'Do you know what he's doing here?' I asked.

Jed said, 'Don't worry about it. I think he's gone again.'

11

My brother Pete was known as a tough guy with a wicked sense of humour. Whenever he was out, he was surrounded; people were drawn to him. Then, at 22, he fell in love. From the moment he met Angela, he was besotted. The tough-guy image, the wildness and petty crookery, he lost interest in it all. Angela was his world.

She was only 17 and was not allowed to sleep at Mum and Dad's house. So, around four o'clock each morning, Pete would walk her home. He was 6-ft-8 and had a huge coat, which he used to button her up inside. Then they would walk along together inside his coat.

Angela and Pete were inseparable. I've never seen two people so in love. She used to warm his socks on top of the fire. When she walked into the room his whole being lit up.

They got engaged on her eighteenth birthday. That night they decided they couldn't bear ever to be apart. They made a pact: if one of them died, the other would die too. They were always chatting; they had great plans for the future. They were going to get a little house and then have two children. When Angela fell pregnant, it disrupted their plans but they were delighted.

When Angela was six months' pregnant, she wanted to live with Pete in Mum and Dad's house. Dad had always had a problem with couples sleeping together under his roof unless they were married.

'I can't condone it,' he told Mum.

'Angela is six months pregnant,' Mum reasoned. 'It's a bit late for worrying, don't you think?'

The day Angela went into labour, Pete called me from the hospital.

'It's started, it's started.'

Four hours later, he called back.

'I don't want Angela to have a baby,' he said. 'She's in too much pain. There's nothing I can do. I feel like I've done something terrible to her.'

'Pull yourself together and get back in there,' I told him sharply.

Three hours later, I had another phone call.

'We've done it. We've got a little girl and she's absolutely beautiful.'

My tough kid brother.

'She's got the Dolan feet,' he informed me.

That meant Pete's daughter had really long toes.

A week after Francesca was born, I popped in to Mum and Dad's. Francesca and Angela were asleep upstairs. I sat with Pete and he said, 'Give me a reading. I haven't had a reading in years.'

We were lounging on the couch with our feet up.

'I'll do a floater,' I said, 'but you know it's hard when I

am close to people. I'll just see what comes.'

I closed my eyes and immediately I saw a vivid moving picture of Pete and Angela. They were going into different pubs in the High Street.

'You're going to go on a pub crawl.'

'Chance'd be a fine thing,' Peter said.

'It must be the weekend,' I told him, 'town looks busy.'

I had a picture of Pete standing up in a crowded pub. Suddenly people were shouting and moving very quickly. At the corner of the picture, I saw a flash of metal. I had words in my head.

'A situation is going to develop that you can't get out of. You are going to go away for a very long time.'

'Clever, sis.' Pete was immediately making a joke of it. He called out to Mum in the kitchen. 'Mia says if I go out for a drink I'll end up in prison.'

The scene was still so strong in my mind. I had a feeling of dread. I opened my eyes and tried to get rid of the picture.

'Listen, Pete,' I said. 'I'm serious.'

'So how long do you expect me to stay in and not go out for a drink?' He was laughing at me.

'I don't know,' I said. 'Three to six months.'

Then he really started laughing. I was just about to try again when Eric's voice came in to my head.

'Leave it,' Eric said. 'You have seen what will be, not what may be.'

Pete continued to make jokes about what I'd said and I tried to smile with him, but I was really worried. I thought of Eric's words. There was nothing I could do.

'The other night, I woke up and saw a tall shadow of a figure standing by the bed. I screwed my eyes up to make sure I was awake, then it was gone,' Pete said. 'Do you think it could have been my guide?'

'It could have been,' I answered. 'The guy I saw next to you was tall and thin.'

'Just think, we could come back as guides next time,' Pete said.

'Do you really think we'd be ready?'

'Whoever dies first out of me and you, let's come back and push the other guide out of the way and become each other's guide,' Pete said. 'We'll have a right crack.'

'I don't think it works like that, Pete,' I said.

He went quiet.

'All right then,' he said. 'Whoever dies first, let's come back and tell the other one what everyone in the family has done that day.'

'All right,' I said, 'you're on. If it's possible, we'll do it.'

We shook hands on it, but in a light-hearted way.

Over the following days, I managed to convince myself Pete would probably get into a fight in a pub, but it wouldn't be serious; no big deal.

Every morning, Pete left Angela in bed and got up with Francesca. He adored the time he spent with her on his own. He did not put her down for a moment. He used to sing to her.

'I never thought I could be a dad – have those feelings,' he told me one morning. 'It overwhelms you, doesn't it?'

His words made me think of my early days with Shane in the intensive care unit. The day we bonded; how it changed my world.

Five weeks after Francesca's birth, a terrible feeling of depression enveloped me. It came out of nowhere. I went into the front room and sat on the couch. There was a lump in my throat; it felt like it would choke me. I knew I was going to cry – the feeling was getting worse and worse.

It was night time; I shut the door in case I woke the children and then I started sobbing. I could not stop for over an hour. I did not know what I was crying about. Eventually, the tears began to subside, but I was still left with a terrible sad feeling. I didn't know what to do with myself. There were scraps of paper on the coffee table that the children had been drawing on. I picked up a pencil and filled the page with words. It was a poem about heaven. I felt better after that.

I went upstairs and washed my face. I couldn't believe what I had just been doing. I stashed all the scraps of paper under the table. Silly scribbles, I thought.

The next day was Pete's twenty-fifth birthday. Pete, Jed and I always got together on our birthdays. It was Saturday so we met in the morning at Mum and Dad's. Jed and I had our children with us. Francesca and Angela were asleep upstairs.

Jed, Pete and I found ourselves together in the front room. It was the first time we had been alone in years. Mum had spent three months knitting Pete a thick, blue fisherman's jumper because he always had trouble finding clothes to fit.

The sleeves were so long they flapped down over his wrists and we were all laughing.

'It's the first time since I was 12 I've had a jumper too big for me,' Pete said.

He rolled up the sleeves. He loved it.

'During the week, an old man fell in the street in front of me,' Jed told us. 'I rushed over to him and he had his eyes open; he looked so scared. Somebody called 999 and I put my arms round him and put his head in the crook of my arm. I said to him, "It's all right mate, the ambulance is on its way, don't worry." He was looking me in the eyes and he died in my arms,' Jed said. 'It was such an awful experience – so awful.'

Pete and I were really quiet, then as usual, Pete made a joke of it.

'One look at you mate,' he said to Jed, 'and the poor bugger had no chance.'

I threw a cushion at Pete.

'Well, I'm not going to reach thirty,' he said.

'Everyone thinks they're not going to get old, Pete,' Jed said.

'No,' he replied. 'I'm serious. I'll die before I'm thirty. I'm going to go out with a bang and hit the headlines.'

'The only way you'll hit the headlines is if the police are involved,' Jed quipped.

We walked into the garden. It was the beginning of October, but the day was sunny. The children were playing in the garden and we watched them.

'When I die, get Mum to throw me on the council tip,' Pete

said. He did not take his eyes off the children. 'You know what she's like, she'll go into debt over the funeral.'

'Don't worry,' Jed said, 'we'll stick you in the wheelie bin.'

'Lighten up, Pete,' I said, 'enjoy your birthday.'

'Don't I always?' he said.

We had a cuddle as I was going, which was unusual.

'Love you,' I said.

'Love you too, sis.'

It was the last time we spoke.

Back at home, I was restless. I could not sit down, I could not relax. I cleaned the house and everything in it – I washed the windows and all the paintwork, I cleared out the toy boxes and washed the net curtains. Everything that could be bleached was bleached.

By 5 p.m. I had done everything that needed to be done indoors, but I was still restless. I needed to be doing something, so I got out the lawnmower and cut the grass. Everything was out of order – that was all I knew; I needed to put it together again.

I cooked dinner for the children and put them to bed, then I tried to still myself by watching television. At 10.20 p.m. there was a knock at the door. It was Mum.

'There's something wrong with Peter,' she said. 'The police are at the house and they want me to go to the police station. I don't want to go on my own.'

As we walked round the corner to Mum's house, she said, 'I can't believe he'd get into trouble, not on his birthday.'

I agreed. 'And not when he's out with Angela.'

I had a terrible feeling. It was more than trouble, I knew it.

A policeman and woman were standing in the front room.

'We really need your Mum to come to the police station,' the police officer said. 'Perhaps you could come with her.'

As he turned to me, we had eye contact. I could feel he was really uncomfortable. I knew then that something bad had happened to Pete, but the policeman didn't want to be the one to tell Mum. I didn't want her to have to go to the police station unless she had to.

'Is he dead?' I asked.

'Mia, don't say that,' Mum tried to quieten me.

'I'm very sorry,' the policeman said, 'he died on the way to hospital.'

Mum collapsed into the armchair and started sobbing.

'You need to go and get my brother,' I told the policeman. I gave him the address. Then I sat on the arm of Mum's chair and put my arm around her. I was very still inside – as if inside of me nothing was happening. It was like being in a dream.

At the back door, I heard Angela's voice.

'Is Peter here?'

I left Mum and went into the hallway to meet her. She was with a friend of Pete's.

'There was a terrible fight, there were men with knives,' Angela said. 'I'm sure Pete got cut by a knife, but he went out of the pub and we can't find him.'

'I'm really sorry Angela' – how to find the words, what to say? – 'Pete died on the way to hospital.'

Angela started screaming. Pete's friend slid down the wall and started sobbing into his hands. I walked Angela into the front room and sat her on the couch. The policewoman looked stressed; she was only young and had probably never done this before.

Angela started rocking backwards and forwards.

'No, no, no, no, no.'

Mum was sobbing. I telephoned the doctor and asked him to come to the house to give them something to help them through. As I put the phone down, Jed arrived with the policeman. Instantly, he heard the sound of Mum and Angela crying.

'What's up? What's going on?'

'Pete is dead.'

Jed went white. He sat with Mum and I was with Angela. They were like wounded animals and there was nothing I could do.

After about 40 minutes, Mum stopped crying, then patted Jed and said, 'I'm all right now.'

Dad had been sleeping through it all. I looked at Jed.

'Leave it for a while,' he said. 'Let him sleep.'

Angela was still wailing. The doctor offered to give her an injection – 'To help you relax.'

She refused; so did Mum.

The policeman called me out into the hallway.

'We need two members of the family to come to the hospital to identify Peter's body.'

'I don't think I can do that.' I had never seen a dead body. I could not look at my brother's corpse.

'If it can't be you and Jed,' he said, 'we'll have to ask your parents.'

No way would I put Mum and Dad through that. I called Jed out into the hallway and told him the situation.

'We'll have to do it,' Jed said. 'There's no choice, is there?'

I did not want to leave Mum and Angela. I kept saying, 'Will you be all right?'

The policewoman offered to stay with them but Mum was clear.

'I think it's better if we're left on our own.'

Mum was uncomfortable in the presence of strangers. Her grief was private.

The hospital was 20 miles away. There was a thick fog. Jed and I held hands in the back of the car the entire journey, but we did not look at each other. We were staring out of different windows.

It was 3 a.m. when we arrived at the hospital. In the relatives' room, they explained that, because Pete's death was a murder enquiry, we had to view the body separately – and not speak until after we had both made a statement confirming Pete's identity.

Jed went into the mortuary first. I was terrified. I did not know what Pete would look like. Would he be disfigured?

'Would you like to come through now?' the hospital worker asked.

I froze in the doorway.

'I'm really sorry,' I said, 'I can't do this.'

The policeman put his hand on my arm.

'I know it's tough,' he said, 'but it's got to be family.'

I took deep breaths and walked in to the room. I froze

again by the door. Pete was lying on a metal bed in the middle of the room. From the shoulders down, he was covered by a cloth.

'You'll have to go a bit closer,' the officer said, 'just quickly.'

I walked over to Pete's body. I stood right next to him. I looked at his face but I could not recognize him. All the features were his, but there was something wrong.

'Can you lower the cloth so I can see the top part of his arm?' I asked.

'Why?'

'I want to see his tattoo – he's got a dodgy tattoo on the top of his arm.'

'You don't know if this is your brother?'

'Will you please just move the cloth?'

There it was: a cartoon snake.

'Yes,' I said. 'It's Pete.'

But it was the husk of Pete. What was missing was the life force. Pete wasn't there.

As we walked past the door to the toilet, I pretended I needed to be sick. Alone inside, I leant my back against the wall. Pete had died suddenly and he was totally in love with Angela and Francesca – he might be confused and try to stay. Like the old woman in Vicki and John's house, he might become a ghost.

'Listen Pete, if you're around, please go over. Don't get stuck,' I spoke to him in my head. 'You can't do anything now. Remember what we talked about. You must go over. I love you.'

When we got back to Mum and Dad's, Angela was asleep on the couch. Dad was awake; he looked grey.

'It was Pete, Mum,' I told her.

I knew she was hoping against hope it was not.

I went home. Tanya had obviously woken in the night and she was in bed with Andy. I got into her bed and, a few minutes later, Shane came to find me.

'I've had a terrible dream,' he told me. 'I dreamt Uncle Jed was dead.'

Tanya had been having a recurring nightmare of a man with a knife and blood all over his hands. Were my children seeing? I still did not know.

'It's all right,' I comforted him. 'Get into bed with me.'

Shane climbed in next to me and I covered us both with the duvet.

The next day we found out how Pete died. He had been in The Railway pub, celebrating his birthday with Angela when a young lad he knew, James, came in looking distraught. James told Pete that he had accidentally jolted a man's beer in another pub. The man head-butted him and broke his nose; he said he was going to kill him. James was only 17; he was terrified and ran to Pete for help.

While Angela was in the toilet, three men came in looking for James. Pete tried to calm the situation. As he turned to the bar, the man pulled a machete from under his coat and hacked Pete three times in the back. Another man picked up a meat cleaver and struck one of Pete's friends in the head.

People were screaming and diving for cover. Pete walked round the corner to the police station to get help. He did not know how badly he had been hurt. At the police station, all he could talk about was Angela.

'Make sure she's okay.'

He would not get into the ambulance until they reassured him that Angela was safe. He died before the ambulance reached the hospital.

Jed went to Sheerness Police Station.

'Is it true you have arrested the guys who killed Peter?'

'Yes we have,' the policeman on the front desk told him.

'They're here?'

'Yes, they're locked up.'

Jed leapt the counter and punched the policeman in the chest. He went flying backwards and Jed found a set of keys. He was fumbling with a key, trying to unlock the door leading to the cells. It took two police officers to pull Jed off. They put him in a cell and called a doctor to give him a tranquillizer. When his rage subsided, he sobbed. They brought him home in a police car; they never charged him.

My grief was quieter. I kept it together because of the deep depression I had gone into the night before Pete died. I had already done my crying. I must have known what was coming – but it was too close for me to take it on consciously.

Pete made the front pages just as he predicted. He had saved the life of a young man and was a hero. Pete's friend with the head injury was in intensive care for many weeks, but made a full recovery.

When you lose someone you've loved all your life, you have so many memories. I remembered when we were kids – trips to the beach, jokes we shared. I remembered his first day at school. I missed Pete in a hundred different ways.

He was gone. It was hard to believe that I was never going to see him again – for all the time I was on Earth. We were never going to share a joke again. There had always been three of us: me, Pete and Jed. Now there was just Jed and I. Loss can rip a family apart, but it pulled Jed and I even closer.

Someone said to me, 'Time is a great healer, you will feel better in time.'

'At least you know you'll see him again,' other people said, referring to my unshakeable belief in life after death.

That faith made it easier, but it didn't take away the loss, the feeling that I missed Pete now. I thought: 'It will never get any better, it is always going to hurt.' But it's true, time heals.

Five weeks after Pete was murdered, a woman called to arrange a party booking at her house. It was time I started working again; it would do me good to be with other people. I arrived at the house relieved that no one there knew anything about my life.

I was shown into a side room. My first client was an 18-year-old girl. When I looked into her eyes, I saw that the biggest problem in her life was an argument she had had with her boyfriend; they had not spoken in a week.

I felt like screaming: 'Problem, you don't know what a problem is.'

I had to work hard not to let her know what I was feeling.

I told her she was going to get back with her boyfriend and somehow managed to finish the reading. I told the other clients I had a headache and left as quickly as I could.

As I got into my car, I thought: 'I can't do this any more.' I started driving. A quarter of a mile from home, I pulled the car into a lay-by and lit a cigarette. Then I heard Eric.

'You're hurting,' he said.

It was the first time he had spoken to me since Pete died.

'Of course I am,' I replied. 'I miss Pete. I'm worrying about Mum and Angela and the children. How can I sit and talk to people about silly things?'

'She was hurting too,' Eric said. 'Because she hasn't experienced the big things, the little things hurt her just as much. It's not her fault she hasn't experienced the same pain as you. How can you judge her? Her pain hurts and that's all that she knows.'

I pictured the girl's earnest face and the desperate look in her eyes. Hers wasn't a massive problem, in the scale of things, but it mattered to her more than anything else in life. She was hurt and lonely. Before Pete died, I would have had total sympathy for her.

'Don't judge other people's pain,' Eric said, 'just feel it.'

I apologized in my mind – to the girl, to Eric. My readings were not just to provide information; they were about standing alongside people in their pain and helping them rise from it.

Later that night, when everyone else was asleep, I asked Eric, 'If I'd stopped Pete going out, could I have stopped him dying?'

'No,' Eric said, 'it was his time.'

'Have we all got a set time?'

'Yes.'

'Can it be changed?'

'No.'

People shouldn't die young, but Eric's words helped me to see that it is not personal – however sad it is for the people left behind.

'Is Pete all right?'

'Of course he's all right.'

'What is he doing?'

'He's resting,' Eric said.

We could not bury Pete's body for three and a half months because there were four post mortems – one for each of the men charged with killing Pete, and one for the Crown. At the funeral, 25 of Pete's friends turned up, all in smart dark suits. Most of them had never owned a suit in their lives. It was beautiful to see.

Angela didn't leave my parents' house for 10 months, apart from going to the shop and back. Mum not only had to grieve the loss of her son, she was constantly worried about Angela and Francesca. Pete and Angela had made a pact never to be parted. Angela wanted to be with him. She wanted to die too.

12

The court case lasted three weeks. Jed and I sat through it all. Fists clenched, I worried he would jump over the dock and attack Pete's murderers. It was so hard to sit there – terrible to hear the extent of the injuries that killed Pete. The machete had gone into his liver, lung and spinal cord. The fact that he managed to walk to the police station to get help for Angela and the others amazed everyone. He died from loss of blood.

Two men were convicted of Pete's murder and were sentenced to life imprisonment; another was sentenced to six years for grievous bodily harm.

After the case, I asked, 'What does life imprisonment mean?'

'They'll be out in about ten years,' a police officer informed me.

'Do you think there should be capital punishment?' the press asked as we left the courthouse.

'No,' I said, 'I don't believe in it. It is premeditated murder. It would make us as bad as the people who committed the crime.'

But the following months were hard. We spent a lot of time

together: Jed, me, Mum, Dad, Angela and the kids. It was a very down time – we all missed Pete so much.

Pete had been dead for about nine months, when I went to the doctor with a prolapsed womb. The gynaecologist said he could do an operation to repair it, but there were no guarantees it would last. I had already been sterilized, so a hysterectomy seemed the most logical step.

I was scared to go into hospital again. The last time I had been there, I had been wrongly given an epidural. What if they messed up again? I talked a lot with the nurses and doctor, made them laugh, tried to make myself memorable. I wanted them to see me as a person, not a body on a conveyor belt. I hoped that would help.

I woke in a bed on the ward, gasping for air. There were nurses around me and machines and drips.

'She's having a reaction to the painkillers,' I heard a nurse say.

Then I went back under.

The next time I opened my eyes, I was propped up on pillows. I saw Pete at the end of the bed. He was smiling at me. I did not know if I was hallucinating or if he was really there. I decided it didn't matter.

'Pete, talk to me,' I said aloud. 'I'm really scared.'

He walked towards me.

'I can't stay and talk,' he said, 'read the book.'

He put a book on my chest.

'I don't want to read a bloody book,' I said. 'Talk to me.'

'I can't stay, sis,' he said again, 'read the book.'

Pete faded away and I looked down at the book. It was a foot square and covered in battered brown leather. Reluctantly I opened it, but instead of pages with words, I saw a swirling picture of a rainforest. As I looked at the trees, I could see they were filled with tiny darts of white light.

The lines of light were thick in the trunks of the trees, thinner in the branches, and more intricate still in the leaves. The trees were filled with life energy. The picture moved downwards so I could see the floor of the forest and the insects. Their bodies and wings, too, were filled with white life force.

Then the page went blank. I licked my finger and, as I turned the page, I saw that I was in the ward. There was no book on my stomach; just my finger in the air. I went back under and the page had been turned. I saw sea life, again filled with darts of life force. Then the plains of Africa and then a city filled with people walking around – all filled with the same life energy.

When I came round fully from the anaesthetic, I felt amazing. I was deeply calm and had a certain knowledge that everything – from a leaf to the most important person in the world – is connected, intrinsically, vitally. The same energy is in everything and we can connect with it all.

Over the next few hours, the feeling of certainty faded, but I was left with an incredible sense of well-being. I went on to have the quickest recovery on the ward and left hospital three days earlier than expected.

One Saturday, 14 months after Pete died, Mum and I went to put flowers on his grave. I was kneeling, arranging the flowers, when a picture flashed into my head of Mum and I at bingo. I stood up.

'We haven't been to bingo in ages,' I said. 'I'd really like to go.'

'I haven't any spare money,' Mum said.

I had only £3 in my purse, but I had never had such a strong urge to play.

'Leave it to me,' I said. 'I'll see if I can raise some money.'

That afternoon, Andy gave me £25 to pay a bill. Borrowing it to play bingo was a huge gamble. What if I lost it? I decided to worry about that next week – if I had to. The next problem was finding a babysitter.

Jed had split up with Theresa and was living with Denise and her baby son, Lee, in a tiny ramshackle flat. He had slipped a disc and was lying in agony on the floor when I arrived. I begged him to let Denise babysit for Shane and Tanya. Then I went out and bought him six cans of beer and put them on the floor beside him. I had to play that night – that was all I knew.

Sheerness Bingo Club was in a shabby hall – the poor man's casino – with bench seats, dingy carpets, Formica tables and peeling magnolia paint, but I felt a rush of excitement.

By the interval, Mum and I had 26 pence left between us. We could only afford one cup of tea, so we shared it. I started to panic about the bill I had to pay on Monday. How was I going to replace the money?

The highlight of the evening was the National, where bingo halls all over the country competed at the same time for the fastest person to get a full house. Mum got one number after another; I stopped looking at my card and concentrated on hers. She was completing her card in no time at all.

'Yes,' I shouted out for her when I saw the final number go down.

We had won the house prize – £60 – that we knew for sure. I had won the money back for the bill, at least, but I knew we had won more than that – possibly the regional prize, maybe even the National.

We had to wait 20 minutes for the result. When the manager offered us a drink, we began to feel optimistic. Then we heard a taped drum roll; this had never happened in the bingo hall before. People stood up, they were looking over at us. The manager climbed on to the stage. Everything seemed in slow motion. I held my breath.

'The Regional Prize was won by a member of the Sheerness Club,' he said.

We had won £5,500. People cheered and clapped, but the manager held his hand up, calling for silence.

'And for the first time in the Club's history,' he continued, 'the National Prize has been won by a member of the Sheerness Club.'

£50,000. The bingo hall erupted. People stood on their chairs, clapping. Pete's murder had been in all the newspapers, together with a picture of Mum at his graveside. People were delighted that something good had happened to us. All Mum and I did was look at each other and smile.

Outside the bingo hall, we got into my battered Cortina, looked at each other and said, 'Ready?'

Then, together, we screamed.

'I can't believe it,' I said. 'A few minutes ago, all we had was 26 pence.'

'You got the idea to go to bingo when you were leaning down by Pete's stone doing the flowers,' Mum said. 'It's a gift from Pete.'

'It must be,' I said. 'I couldn't explain it, but I had such a compulsion to play.'

And then I told her what I'd done. 'I even used the money Andy gave me to pay the gas bill,' I said.

We could not stop grinning.

'Cheers, Pete,' we both said.

Mum and I always share our winnings. We decided to give the £5,500 Regional Prize to Jed and drove straight round to see him. It took him ages to haul himself off the floor and get to the front door. When he heard our news, he took a while to believe it. Then he was alternately smiling and wincing in pain.

Andy and Denise were waiting for me in the front room.

'You're late,' Andy said.

'We went to see Jed because' – I paused for effect – 'tonight Mum and I won the National.'

'What does that mean?'

Andy was not a bingo player, he had no idea.

'We won £55,500.'

'Hold on,' Andy said immediately, 'what day is it?' He looked at his watch. 'It's April the first tomorrow,' he said triumphantly. 'I'm not going to be your April fool.'

I had no paperwork, nothing to show that I was telling the truth. It took me ages to convince him that we had really won.

When the cheque arrived, 10 days later, I went with Mum to deposit it at the bank. Perennially overdrawn and terrified of the bank manager, it was the only time in her life the bank manager offered her a cup of tea. Timidly, Mum asked how long it would be until she could draw money out.

'I can let you have some money now,' he said and gave her £1,000 in cash.

10.30 a.m. and our purses were full of money we never expected to have.

'£500 each,' Mum said. 'Let's go shopping.'

I bought a toy each for Shane and Tanya and aftershave for Andy, but I was totally unable to spend money on myself. After an hour, Mum had only managed to buy a bra and a roll of bin bags.

We had been so long without money, we did not know what to do with it. I had never known Mum eat in a restaurant, so we treated ourselves to spaghetti bolognese. Sitting in that little Italian restaurant in Chatham, we planned a summer holiday with the children. There had been so much pain in our lives but that day we were happy.

A few weeks later, we went shopping again.

'I bet I can spend a grand quicker than you can,' Mum dared me.

'I bet you can't.'

We arranged to meet in an hour. I managed to buy a leather coat, boots, jeans, jumpers and a watch. But Mum won – she bought a bedroom suite. She waved the receipt at me triumphantly.

Jed came with us on that shopping trip – equipped with a walking stick and a weightlifting belt to support his back. He bought a suit – his first really good suit – and a three-piece suite and dining room table and chairs. The rest of the money, he spent on moving his family from their grotty one-bed flat to a small house. £5,500 changed their lives dramatically.

Over the next weeks, life with Andy improved too. He had been very stressed about bills, but with the pressure off, he was less irritable – more light-hearted. He began to lark about with the kids. He stopped shouting.

The money shifted the balance of power between us too. The house was in a real mess, full of stuff that was broken and on its last legs. I spent money on getting the house done up: new sink units, cupboards, carpets, MFI bedroom units for the kids. It was my money so, for the first time in my life, I chose.

Money can't buy you happiness, but it can buy you choices. Now I could afford for the kids to join clubs, they were having a wonderful time. They were members of the swimming club, they went roller skating and played tennis. They loved it.

Mum and I spent some of our winnings on taking Shane and Tanya to Butlins. I had never had a holiday; neither had Shane and Tanya – and we had new clothes and money to spend. When we arrived, we had to queue at reception, so I had a go on the one-armed bandit next to me. I put a pound coin in the slot and, on the third press of the button, all the lights and bells started up.

'How much did you put in?' a man asked me.

'A pound,' I said, as £250 in coins gushed out of the bandit and onto the floor. One of the Butlins staff brought me a blue cloth moneybag and we scooped up my winnings.

'Spending money,' I beamed at Mum, as we split the winnings between us.

'Can we go on the fairground rides?' Shane asked. There were giant Disney characters there; he had never seen anything like it.

'Yes,' I said. 'You can go on everything.'

That night, as we were walking through the fairground, we came across a bingo hall.

'Shall we?' I asked Mum. 'Quickly?'

We bought six tickets each. On the last game, Mum got a full house. It was the last game of the night. She won £300. We had only been at Butlins a few hours and already we had won £550. It was surreal. We had the Midas touch.

Over that week, Mum and I won at bingo several times. We had a wonderful week, bought loads of rubbish souvenirs and still came home with more money than we had spent.

Over the next months, Mum and I went to bingo every fortnight. We won the £1,000 Link Prize four times, and countless other prizes. Andy began his own horticultural business. He was happier, more light-hearted. He felt better about himself. So much was changing.

I also received a letter from the solicitor I had consulted about the epidural incident. My claim against the Health

Authority had been dragging on for seven years but now he wrote to advise me that the Health Authority wanted me to see a psychologist.

'They want to try to find out the affect the epidural had on your mental state,' he told me.

It looked like there might be a breakthrough at last. Just don't mention anything to do with clairvoyance, I warned myself. I needed to appear normal – as normal as anyone can.

'I'm a psychologist, but I'm also the chairwoman for the Society for Registered Hypnotherapists,' the psychologist told me. 'I'd like to put you under mild hypnosis so you are more relaxed,' she said. 'Would that bother you?'

'No,' I said, thinking it might be interesting.

I went into the hypnotic state easily; I was relaxed – so relaxed I did not care what I said.

'I want you to tell me what you remember about your eighth birthday,' the psychologist said.

Instead of seeing eight-year-old Mia, I saw a greenhouse with broken windows and a one-eyed Siamese cat. I told her exactly what I saw. Then she snapped her fingers and brought me round. I realized then what I had done – I had given her a reading.

'How do you know I've got a one-eyed Siamese cat and that the glass blew off my greenhouse?'

'I'm very sorry,' I said, attempting to play it down. 'I just have an ability to see things. I didn't mean to intrude.'

The psychologist was fascinated and wanted to write a paper on me. So I went to see her several times. A month later, she sent a report saying I was a strong character with sound mind and high morals. It was a great report. Two months later, my solicitor telephoned to say that, after seven years, we finally had a court date.

The morning before the case, the Health Authority offered me £10,000 to drop the case. I refused. In the afternoon, I got an offer of £20,000.

The solicitor said, 'I think you should take it.'

I refused. Six o'clock that evening, the Health Authority offered me £30,000.

'I think you should take it,' the solicitor said again. 'The law says if the judge awards you one penny less in court, you will get nothing.'

It is a stupid law, but I accepted the out-of-court settlement and purchased our council house with the money. Then our winning streak – Pete's gift – stopped just as suddenly as it had started.

One morning, as I was opening the bedroom curtains, I saw my grandmother Grace's face clearly in my head. Something was wrong – she was worried. I had to go and see her. Grace and Arthur only lived a few miles away, but I had not been to their house in years. I saw Grace at Mum's house and she occasionally visited me, but I did not want to see Arthur. That made the house taboo.

Grace did not have a telephone so, after I dropped the children at school, I drove to her house. She opened the door straightaway. She was wearing a checked housecoat and slippers. She looked old and vunerable.

'I'm so glad to see you, I've been so worried,' she said.

'Arthur's not well and he won't go to the doctor. I don't know what to do.'

From the doorway, I could see him. He was bent forward in an armchair, looking shrunken and frail. He was gazing at the floor, and I was standing at the door looking at him. I did not want to go near.

But I had to talk to him – he was clearly in a lot of pain. I walked across the room and squatted by his chair. I pushed all my feelings out of the way; I had to be neutral.

'Arthur,' I said. 'You're not well.'

He lifted his head from his hands and turned to look at me. His skin was yellow and there was terrible pain in his eyes. His face was so drawn.

'I've got backache,' he said.

I went to the payphone and telephoned the doctor. He told me to bring Arthur to the surgery right away. He was so ill and Grace was very worried, somebody had to do something. I had no choice.

Arthur shuffled towards my car. It took him ages, but I did not help him, I did not want to touch him. I opened the car door and he struggled to bend down. He was in pain – I told myself off for being selfish – he needed assistance – I put my hand under his elbow and guided him into the car.

At the reception desk, I was asked, 'Who are you in relation to Arthur?'

Before I could answer, Arthur said, 'She's my niece.'

I did not want to contradict him; I said nothing. He wanted me to go in with him to see the doctor, so I sat there while the doctor listened to Arthur's chest. Then he lifted Arthur's shirt and I saw his stomach and chest. He was covered in lumps the size of marbles. He must have been in a lot of pain.

'I'd like you to wait outside while I have a word with your niece,' the doctor said.

Arthur had secondary cancer, too far gone to be treated. He was dying. I could not believe I was the one hearing it.

'In cases like this, if he asks directly we'll tell him,' the doctor said, 'but if he doesn't ask, we won't.'

'How long will he live?'

'It's a matter of weeks.'

I took Arthur to the hospital and hung around while they found him an airbed and put him on a morphine drip. He had no fight left. I tried to keep my voice light.

'I'm going to go and get some of your things,' I told him.

'Will you come back?' His voice was desperate.

'Yes,' I said. 'I'll come back in a few hours.'

I rang Mum and we discussed how to tell Grace. He had been her companion for nearly 30 years. We went to her house together to break the news. She wept and wept. She couldn't go to the hospital. She did not want to lie to him and she could not bear to watch him slip away.

'It's all right,' Mum consoled her. 'We'll sort it out.'

Outside, Mum confided that she did not think she could sit with someone while they died – and she was at work all day. She had no idea what Arthur had done to me and I couldn't tell her, not then.

'I'll visit him,' I said.

The next day, I dropped the children off at school and went to see Arthur. He was sleeping, so I sat by his bed and started reading a magazine. Suddenly he woke up and held his hand out towards me. I took it.

'Are you all right, Arthur?'

He looked at me. His eyes were cloudy.

'Sorry,' he said.

I felt as if he had punched me. My head was filled with images of what he'd done to me as a child – flash, flash, flash, memory after memory. Then the images stopped. I looked at him; he was a shrivelled old man in terrible pain. I felt: it's over, it's finished.

'It's all right,' I said.

I sat by Arthur's bed every day for two weeks. I could not bear the thought of him dying alone and there was no one else to sit there. So, each morning, after I dropped the children at school, I spent my day at the hospital.

As I walked up the stairs to the ward each morning, I felt tense. Many times I had to leave his bedside and go outside to have a cigarette to relieve the knot in my stomach. I did not want to be there, but I felt I had no choice.

He was mainly unconscious. I asked myself: would I have wished this pain on him? I looked deep inside to see what I honestly felt. I was not judging him, I was just there. But sitting with him hour after hour was hard.

One day I came out of the ward, got into my car and put my head on the steering wheel. I wanted someone to know what I was going through. In that instant, I wanted to talk to Mum, but he was dying and it was in the past. It was not the time to tell. Besides, I told myself, he was not the person he used to be. I was sitting with an old man who was dying and scared.

The nurses had my telephone number in case of an emergency in the night. The call came at nine o'clock; Arthur was dying. Mum stayed with the children. I went alone.

He was in a little side room. It was very quiet. I was shown to a chair by his bed and I watched his chest and ribs rising and falling, his hands limp on the sheet. I picked up the hand nearest to me and I held it between mine.

I sat there, like that, for nearly an hour. Then something in the room changed. The air was electric. I knew something was happening but I didn't know what it was. I was still holding Arthur's hand and it felt as if he was way down deep inside his body. Then I felt his spirit start to rise, the energy in his hand got lighter and lighter. His eyes opened and he turned his head to look at me and smiled very softly. Then he died. I could feel his energy going on up.

I let go of Arthur's hand and looked up. The air was filled with shimmering lights. I was in awe, full of wonder and peace. Tears streamed down my face. The nurses came in; they thought my tears were sadness.

'It's best he's gone,' a nurse said, 'he was in terrible pain.'

I could not explain that I was crying because of the mystery of someone dying. It had been an honour to be there. I looked back up at the ceiling and the lights had gone.

After Arthur died, Grace and I went through his things. We discovered that, as a member of a parachute regiment in the Second World War, he had saved countless lives and been awarded medals. There were papers commending him on deeds of heroism. He had never told anyone.

I thought about all the lives Arthur saved. Then I thought that you can't judge a person's whole life on one deed. Just because someone does something bad, does not mean that they are not capable of good. A lot of people do things they regret and feel remorse for the rest of their lives; they consider themselves bad people. But good balances out the bad. Nothing is black and white. I contacted the local parachute regiment and, at his funeral, Arthur received a Guard of Honour.

13

Pete had been dead for two years when I saw him again. I was doing a reading, telling a woman what the spirit of her dead mother was saying, when I saw Pete standing behind her. He was as clear and as real as she was.

'All right, sis?' he said.

He smiled and I saw the same mischievous grin on his face. I was torn. I desperately wanted to talk to my kid brother, but I needed to give comfort to the woman grieving in front of me.

'Pete, give me half an hour,' I said.

He nodded.

When Pete came back, I asked him, 'Are you okay?'

'I am now,' he said. 'But I was freaked out when I found myself dead.'

'What's it like to die?'

'I seemed to come back every few days. I saw everyone grieving, but my visits were so short. Now it's as though I've been to sleep for a long time.'

His personality was the same – I looked in his eyes and I knew it – he had lost nothing, but there was something different. When he was alive, he was all over the place, but now he was totally calm. There was a serenity coming off him.

I wanted to talk and ask more questions but Pete said, 'I haven't got much time, let me tell you what Mum and the family have been doing today.'

The pact we made – he remembered.

'Mum dropped her car keys down the drain at work,' Pete said. 'Jed got a bruise on the back of his hand from a machine at work and Dad heard from his brother.'

I wrote it all down.

'Are you all right?' I asked again.

'Yes, I'm okay.' He was fading. 'I've got to go.'

As soon as I recovered, I telephoned Jed.

'Did you hurt your hand at work today?' I asked.

'Yeah,' he said. 'How do you know, you witch?'

'It's not me,' I said. 'Pete came through.'

Jed was quiet. He was dubious about clairvoyance; he'd never asked for a reading.

Eventually, he asked, 'What did Pete say?'

'He said you hurt the back of your hand at work.'

'Is he all right?'

'He seemed great, Jed.'

'You really did speak to him?'

'Yes,' I said. 'I did.'

Then I telephoned Mum.

'Did you drop your keys down the drain?'

'I did actually,' she said, 'but they landed on the grate and I just managed to catch them.'

'Did Dad speak to his brother?'

'How do you know that?'

'Pete came through and told me.'

She went quiet, so I told her exactly what had happened.

'Did he seem all right?'

'He seemed really relaxed.'

The next night, Mum asked me to see if I could talk to Pete again. I didn't want to disappoint her.

'It's taken more than two years to get the silly bugger through the first time,' I said. 'What are the chances of being able to pick him up the next day?'

But that night, the clairvoyant space came easy and clear. Eric arrived.

'Emotions cloud clairvoyance,' he said.

I saw Pete's face in my mind. I felt a wave of conflicting emotions, at which he started to fade. I took a deep breath, calmed myself, and Pete came back into focus.

'Hello Mum,' he said looking at her.

I told her what he'd said.

'Ask Pete what I did before coming to yours tonight,' she said.

Mum knows the closer I am to someone the harder it is to give clairvoyance. Her question was a test. I looked at Pete.

'This is important Pete,' I said. 'Please tell me.'

Pete smiled and faded once more. In his place I saw a piece of polished wood with a silver disc at its centre. It made no sense to me, so I tried again. I told Mum what I was seeing, but eventually I broke off, exasperated and disappointed.

I brought my attention back to the living room.

'I'm sorry I wasn't able to answer your question,' I said.

Mum shook her head. There were tears in her eyes.

'Before coming to your house tonight,' she said, 'I sat quietly on my own and asked Pete, if he was really okay, to give me a sign that nobody in the world could know. Then I pulled that old silver dollar out of my bag and placed it in the centre of my coffee table ...'

Pete's death had shaken Mum but, from that night on, she started to come back to her old self. She would never stop missing Pete, but to know your child is okay, even if he's away from you, makes everything else bearable.

Andy wanted to leave the island and move into the country. I was used to having Mum and Dad round the corner and I resisted as long as I could, but Andy was becoming irritable again. I hoped the move would lighten his spirits.

He found a farmhouse in Tonge, 10 miles from the island. It was in the middle of nowhere. The night we moved in, I stood in the garden and watched night fall. It was totally black. I'd always lived in streets with lamps and other houses, but in Tonge there was nothing but us and the darkness. I came inside and shut the door.

For the first months, I felt very isolated. Shane had been diagnosed with numerical dyslexia and during the week he boarded at a specialist school in Margate. At first he came home every weekend, then, increasingly, he wanted to stay at school with his friends.

Andy was out a lot, running his own horticultural business.

With no family around to look after Tanya, I was house-
bound. After picking her up from school at 3.30 each afternoon, we were in the farmhouse, together, for the rest of the
night. When she went to bed around nine, I watched TV and
waited for Andy to come home. I had no one to talk to.

I missed having Mum and Dad round the corner, I
missed popping in to see Jed and Denise. One afternoon,
I was driving Tanya home from school, when we saw a
notice advertising horse-riding lessons. Tanya started having
lessons and, slowly, we began to make friends and have a
social life.

The riding school had to close down. Tanya was distraught
at the thought of leaving her favourite pony, Jimby, so on the
spur of the moment I bought him. We moved him to stables
and we became involved in the equestrian world; I even ended
up being a commentator at show-jumping events.

Clients started to travel to see me for readings. A new client
came. He was in his late fifties and wearing a very smart dark
blue three-piece suit. He was balding, with hair around the
sides of his head. I gave him a reading, providing information
about the pubs he owned and his marriage, but I kept thinking there was something about his life I wasn't getting. He was
a nice guy with a happy marriage and no financial problems;
I knew there was something else, but no matter how I looked
I couldn't see what it was.

At the end, I asked, as I always do, 'Is there something you
want to ask me?'

'Can I show you some photographs?'

'Of course,' I said.

He opened his briefcase, took out a Kodak packet and handed it to me. I expected to see photographs of his family. Instead, the first photograph was of him in a long pink dress. He was wearing a curly blonde wig, make-up and high heels.

Stalling for time and trying to regain my composure, I carried on looking at the photographs. In each, he was wearing a different dress and wig. The gowns were amazing creations with little bolero jackets and silk flowers. The photos were not suggestive or sexy; he looked like Mrs Doubtfire in a posh frock.

'They're lovely dresses,' I said at last. I looked back up to his face. 'What would you like to ask me?'

'Do you think it's bad?' he asked.

I looked at him. I knew dressing up was his secret; I knew it had nothing to do with anyone else. He needed somebody to tell him it was all right.

'It's not a bad thing to do,' I said. 'There is nothing wrong in it, but your wife doesn't know and I think she might be shocked if she found out, so try to be sensible about it.'

'So, it's not bad?' he asked again.

'No,' I said. 'It does not make you a bad person.'

He gathered his photos up and thanked me. Then, this man who looked like a bank manager, walked out of my house and back to his life.

Gradually, Andy's moodiness resurfaced. The farmhouse had not changed anything inside him. His temper started to blow.

I was always on edge. Even when he was being nice, I was on tenterhooks, waiting for the explosion.

Dinner was a focal point of his fury. Each morning I was stressed about what to cook for him that evening, but he would never tell me what he wanted. I invariably got it wrong. Worse still were the times I did not get dinner on the table at the time specified. He was always demanding, criticizing, angry about something, hurling dinner plates across the kitchen, twisting my stomach into knots.

One night, my friend Belinda came to have dinner with us. I made a big macaroni cheese and served it with side salad and crusty bread. Suddenly, he slammed his fork on the plate. My heart went. Surely he was not going to do this in front of Belinda?

'I'm not eating this crap.'

He stood up so quickly the chair went over behind him. He stormed up the stairs; we could hear him: bang, bang, bang.

'Shit,' I said, 'he's gone into one.'

Shane was boarding at school and Tanya was in bed. Usually, I would have fled, but I was embarrassed in front of Belinda. I wanted to play it down. Upstairs we could hear him shouting and swearing. Then there was a loud smash, the sound of glass breaking and a crash outside on the drive. We got up and walked to the front door. The portable TV was a mess on the drive. I looked up. The bedroom window was smashed; he had thrown the TV out of it.

'I think you had better go,' I told Belinda.

'He's mad,' she said. 'Are you going to be all right?'

I did not want Belinda to see how frightened I was.

'Yes,' I said, 'I'm fine.'

As soon as Belinda was out of sight, I grabbed my cigarettes and lighter and ran into the orchard. I sat with my back against a tree. In the moonlight, the trees were like silver skeletons. I thought how, when I first moved here, the darkness scared me. Now nothing in the darkness could scare me as much as what was inside the house. When the bedroom light went off at midnight, I went back inside.

I fled to the orchard countless times. Sometimes it was freezing but I never went back until I felt confident Andy had calmed down.

'You over-react,' he always said afterwards. 'You need to see a shrink and sort out your head.'

I'd lay beside him in bed, tense with fear. If I moved, he'd snap, 'Can't you fucking well keep still, I'm trying to sleep.' I was too scared to move. One day I bought a single bed for the spare room. I told Andy it was for the nights I couldn't sleep. The room was big enough only for the bed and a tiny table with a lamp, but I felt safe in there.

One night I woke and Andy had his hand around my throat; his other hand was over my mouth.

'Wake up,' he hissed.

My heart was thundering.

'Get up,' he said and started dragging me down the stairs. The situation was made more bizarre by the fact we were both being quiet so that we did not wake the kids.

Andy dragged me into the front room and pinned me up

against the wall. He had his hand around my throat. The room was in darkness. His face was only a few inches from mine. My mind was racing: 'What could be the matter? What was going on?'

'That fucking dinner you cooked ...'

Dinner? That was eight hours earlier ...

'It was shit,' Andy said. 'You don't give a toss about me.'

He's insane, I thought. I remembered that he had eaten it.

'I can't take much more of this,' he said. 'You wind me up all the time.'

Eventually he let me go. I was only wearing a short night-dress but I ran out the back door and into the trees again. It was 2 a.m. I stayed there until dawn, rocking backwards and forwards. I was terrified. Somebody help me. Eric, help me, please.

'Have patience,' Eric said.

After that, each night, I used to wedge a dining room chair under the door handle of my little room.

One day, at the end of a reading, a woman pushed a photo-graph across the table towards me.

'Can you tell me anything about the person in this photo, please?'

I started to say, 'Actually I don't work with photographs,' when I looked at the photo and locked eyes with the man in it. It was as if the eyes were alive – they were full of emotion. I was engrossed. I had images of him doing build-ing work.

'Is he a builder?'

'Yes.'

This was a whole new aspect – a door to a new room. I saw him putting his arm around her.

'It's your partner.'

'Yes.' She grinned.

After she had gone, I got out my photographs and looked at the eyes. If I looked at friends in old photos, I could pick up how they were now. Then I looked at a photo of Pete; there was a difference in the eyes – they seemed flat and lifeless. That's how I discovered I could work from photos.

Another morning, a smart, well-spoken man in his fifties arrived at my door. As soon as I started his reading, I could see his aura was heavier on one side than the other. That meant either depression or stress. I started the health scan and that confirmed it for me.

As I went into his personality, I saw images of him in sexual acts with little boys. They were only six or seven years old. I was revolted. I wanted to stop the reading and get him out of my house.

I closed my eyes, frantically calling for Eric.

'I can't do this,' I told him. 'How do I get rid of him?'

Eric's voice seemed to take ages to come through.

'It's not for you to judge,' he said.

I was supposed to be neutral emotionally, I knew that. I made an excuse and left the room. Upstairs I smoked a cigarette and paced the floor. I decided to go back and finish the reading, but not mention the images I saw. I didn't know how I could talk about them with him – how could I feel mother love for someone who sexually abused children?

I went into the room. As I went back into his personality, I saw him crying with his head in his hands. I knew he had thought about taking his life. Revulsion mixed with pity – a part of me felt sorry for him, for his terrible depression and pain.

I gave him practical information about his work and finances. At the end, I was going to stop, but suddenly I had words in my head that I had to give him.

'I can feel you've been very depressed and I know your weakness. You're considering an option that's been given to you. It will be brave to do it. You can go forward and do good things to outweigh the bad things you've done. But only you can make the decision.'

I opened my eyes and looked at him. I knew he had spent time in prison for sexual offences against children.

'I've been offered an experimental injection that stops sexual urges,' he said. 'I've been warned that there are side effects, but I don't know of any other option.'

'Someone has to be first,' I said. 'Helping out with the experiment is doing something good.'

He started to cry.

'Thank you so much for seeing me.'

I shook his hand. I was confused. I was repulsed by his actions but I felt sorry for him. When he left, I thought about the fact he spent much longer being depressed and in pain than he did in abusing children. I realized it would be easy to consider him – and all those like him – monsters, but he knew he was doing wrong. He was scared of himself. It was another reminder to see beyond a person's actions, to look for the cause rather than write anybody off.

A girl booked in for a reading. As soon as she arrived, I knew there was something not quite right about her. I started the health scan and saw confusion around her. She was in her early twenties and lived with her parents, but she didn't trust them. I saw hospitals and medication. I saw an isolated and paranoid world.

Eric came into my head.

'Take it easy,' he said. 'Be careful.'

'I want you to connect me with my higher self,' she said suddenly. 'I want to talk to her.'

'Your higher self isn't someone else,' I explained, 'she's you, within you.'

But she was not listening; she had a glazed look on her face.

'You're a disciple, aren't you?' she said, 'like Christ.'

I was horrified.

'No,' I said. 'Not at all.'

'But you know things about people, like a disciple.'

'There are loads of people like me,' I said, trying to lighten the tone.

She was delusional and I knew my ability as a psychic was useless to her. She was only hearing what she wanted to hear. I spent the last half hour of our session, trying to convince her to go back to see her doctor.

'You don't have to feel like this,' I told her.

She took ages to leave. In the end, I drove her to the railway station and refused any money for the reading.

I knew I mustn't take another booking from her. I could not help.

She started phoning at different hours of the day and night, asking obscure questions and trying to keep me talking. Then, two weeks later, she turned up at my door.

'What are you doing here?' I asked. 'You haven't got an appointment.'

'I know,' she said, 'but I wanted to be near you. I feel safe near you. If I can't come in, I'll just sit in the garden.'

I made her a cup of tea and dropped her back at the train station. She grabbed my hand.

'You're such a special person,' she said.

She had a dreamy look on her face.

'I'm not,' I tried to tell her again. 'I'm just ordinary. I really think you should go back to see your doctor.'

She turned up at the house four more times. Each time, she arrived in a taxi and I took her back to the station. The last time, I did not answer the door. She kept banging and calling for me through the letterbox. I felt guilty, but I knew she had to have a bad experience of coming to see me, otherwise she would never stop.

Eventually, from the top window, I watched her walk away. Then the phone calls started up, four and five times a day; she was crying and pleading.

'Can I come to see you, Mia? I feel safe with you. I won't be a problem, I'll help you, I'll do the housework.'

I was always kind to her, but I felt helpless and out of my depth. The children were frightened to pick the phone up in case it was her. One day she started calling early and, by teatime, I had had a dozen calls from her. I stopped answering the phone. At 2 a.m., it rang again.

'Mia,' she said, 'I'm at the police station. They said they'll let me go if I've got a safe house to go to. I told them my safe house is where you are.'

'Wait,' I said. 'Wait ...'

'I'm going to give the phone to the police officer so you can tell him where you live and he can bring me to you.'

She had been stalking me for three months; it was late at night. I lost my temper.

'You're not coming to my house,' I shouted. 'I don't want to see you or speak to you again.'

I put the phone down and burst into tears. I felt I'd done something terribly wrong. She was lost and confused and I was nasty to her, but I didn't know what else to do.

'You can't help everybody,' Eric said.

But, deep inside, I felt I'd failed.

That summer, a man came to see me for a reading, but before I started, he said, 'I'd like to explain the reason I'm here and get straight to the point.'

He put a photograph of a woman on the table in front of me.

'I've come about my wife,' he said. 'She's been missing for three weeks. I know she's alive. I just want to know where she is.'

I looked down at the photo and saw his wife's eyes clearly. I knew she was dead.

'So,' I said cautiously, 'you want to know where she is?'

'Yes,' he said, 'can you help me?'

I said, 'I can try.'

He laid a few pieces of jewellery in front of me.

'I thought these might help,' he said.

I felt very uncomfortable. I picked up a ring and closed my eyes, frantically wondering what to say. I couldn't tell him his wife was dead. I saw a big cream square building with an expanse of neat, clipped lawn, shrubs and undergrowth. I told him what I saw.

'The only strong picture is the undergrowth,' I said. Then I got the words, 'She won't come back to you, but you'll find out where she is before Christmas.'

He did not want to know any more. After he had gone, I thought about the place I had seen. I knew it was the local cricket ground at Gore Court. Should I go and check whether she was there? What would I do if I found her? Andy's mum lived close to the cricket ground, so I asked her to look.

'The undergrowth was so dense, I couldn't get in,' she reported.

Six months later, I heard a news flash on the radio. A body had been found at Gore Court Cricket Ground. The next day, the local paper was filled with it. The undergrowth was dying back as winter was coming on; that's how the woman's body was discovered. She had been murdered the summer before. I wished, then, I had had the courage of my convictions and gone to the cricket ground to find her. I felt very guilty that, for all those months, I had left her there.

Andy's irrational violence was gathering momentum. The threat was always there that he would punch me again. The not knowing was a torture. He might as well have hit me; my body winced when I was near him. It still amazes me how much terror a person can put up with for so long.

Andy used to grab me by the hair and throat. Once he put a screwdriver up against my throat because I refused to have sex with him. His rage was terrifying. He was out of control.

He would sweep his arm along the kitchen top, smashing everything on it. One day, he dragged the drawers out of the chest and hurled the contents against the walls. He had his hand up against my throat again. I thought he was going to kill me. Terrified, I fled into the orchard and then walked all the way to Sittingbourne to get away from him. I walked for three hours. When I got there, I telephoned Belinda. I had no money, so I reversed the charges.

She came to collect me, took me to a café for coffee and bought me a packet of cigarettes.

'You can't carry on like this,' she said.

'I don't know how I can get away from him,' I confessed. 'He said he'll kill me if I try to take Tanya.'

A few hours later, she dropped me back. Yet again Andy told me that I had over-reacted. He never apologized. Then, as usual, he gave me money to replace the things he had broken.

'I think you need to get some more bits and pieces,' he said.

The turning point came on Shane's fifteenth birthday.

I was in the kitchen, preparing a special supper, when Andy came in and told me, 'You do know, when Shane's sixteen, he's got to move out.'

I was speechless. He was telling me that he expected me to turn my own son out of the house. I realized, in that moment, that I had stayed with Andy and put up with all his cruelty because the children were safe and had everything they needed. That was a reason for enduring. Now he was turning on Shane. Something hardened inside me.

A week later, Andy got into a temper. Instead of running from him, for the first time since he punched me, I felt totally calm. I slowly walked into the hallway and put on my coat and boots. Then I walked into the kitchen and collected my purse, cigarettes and bag. I got into my car and went to pick Tanya up from school. All of a sudden, I didn't care what Andy did.

'We're going to stay the night at Nan and Grandad's,' I told her.

Tanya was delighted. At 12, she had never spent a night at my parents' house because Andy wouldn't allow it.

An hour later, I telephoned Andy.

'I'm not coming back tonight,' I told him. 'I'll see you tomorrow. I've got Tanya.'

He started threatening and screaming abuse at me, but I had no fear.

'Do whatever you want,' I said. 'I'll see you tomorrow.'

Then I put the phone down.

That night, Tanya and I shared the bed in the spare room. I lay awake beside her knowing that I was leaving Andy. When he said Shane had to leave home, I lost my reason for staying. The children weren't safe. I couldn't tell myself any longer that I was staying with him for their benefit.

I was leaving Andy, but this time I was not going to run off. I was going to confront him head on. No matter what he did to me, I was still going to go. I'd been scared so many times, but I no longer had it in me to be scared. I'd rather take the punishment than live with the constant fear that it was going to happen. I knew I couldn't live my old life any more. I felt fatalistic. Whatever would be would be.

The next morning, I told Mum I was leaving Andy, then I went back to the farmhouse. As soon as I walked in, Andy started shouting.

'If you take my daughter away again,' he said, 'I'll break your legs.'

I walked into the kitchen and put the kettle on. I made two cups of tea and put them on the coffee table in the lounge. He was still berating me, but I felt so different, so calm. For years, I'd prayed for something to happen to help me get away from Andy, but I knew now, it had to be me. Fourteen-and-a-half years to reach that conviction.

'I'm leaving you,' I said. 'I can't live with you anymore. It's over.'

'If you think you're taking my daughter away from me …'

I looked at him and I knew he couldn't look after Tanya – he never had. I called his bluff.

'You have Tanya then,' I said. 'Whatever happens, I am leaving.'

Andy's horticultural business was doing well. He thought he could use it to bargain with me.

'What do you think you're going to do?' he said derisively.

'You can't manage without me.'

'I'll rent somewhere.'

'You're not having the furniture.'

'It doesn't matter.'

'You can't afford to live on your own.'

'I'll do more readings.'

'You won't make anywhere near the sort of money you're used to.'

'You haven't got a clue,' I told him. 'Money doesn't mean a thing. I would rather live in a tent.'

Then suddenly, strangely, Andy changed his mind.

'Perhaps it's a good idea,' he said. 'But I think you should get a place near here, so I can see Tanya when I want to.'

He'd given Tanya back to me.

'All right,' I said.

14

It took four weeks to find a cottage and move out of the farm-house. During that time, Andy veered from wanting me to stay to wanting me to go. One day I could take Tanya, the next I could not. I never wavered. I had a new strength. I couldn't live with him anymore. For a month, I was on tenterhooks. Then on 11 February 1994 I moved to a new life – just the children and me.

The first night was freezing. I spent three hours trying to light the Rayburn in the kitchen and failed miserably. So I lit a coal fire in the tiny front room and put the children's mat-tresses on the floor in front of it. Then we went out and bought fish and chips, chocolate biscuits and cans of coke and had them on the floor in front of Tanya's portable TV.

A few hours earlier, we had been in a big farmhouse equipped with every comfort. Now the three of us were in a tiny room with a curtain improvised out of a sheet, but this was the first happy night I'd had for a long, long time.

I woke in the morning and I felt so light. It took a few moments to realize what this feeling was – it was the absence of fear.

The cottage had not been decorated for 20 years, so Jed came with Alan, a friend of Pete's, and they painted the house. Belinda came too, and made curtains. The house was bustling and chaotic and filled with laughter, the way I liked it.

It took five weeks to do up the house and over that time Alan and I grew closer and closer. I liked being near him. We had known each other since childhood – he was always around Pete, so always at our house. He was the one person I considered sleeping with when I first discovered Andy's infidelity. He was kind and gentle and, after 14½ years of Andy, he was a breath of nourishing air.

One night I cooked dinner and he said, 'I'll wash up – it's only fair.'

Andy hadn't washed a plate in all the time we were together. I was relearning what was normal between people. I was taking on board how totally abnormal life with Andy had become.

Alan was so easy to be around. There was no strain. No longer living with someone who was about to explode, I was finding a new me. The simplest things gave me great pleasure: living on sandwiches, leaving the washing up in the sink, throwing a crisp packet on the floor.

One evening, we were relaxing in the front room, when Alan said, 'I don't understand about this clairvoyant stuff. I'm not sure I believe in it.'

'Shall I give you a mini reading?' I offered, 'and see what happens?'

I opened up and Pete came through straightaway. He had been one of Alan's best mates; they had known each other since the age of 12.

'Pete's here,' I said.

He looked at me; he clearly did not believe it.

'Ask him to tell me something only he and I know.'

'Tell him about the game of cards,' Pete said, 'where he lost his flat to me for a week.'

I said this to Alan and he got up quickly from the table and backed away.

'Fuck me, he's here, isn't he?'

'I told you he was.'

'Yeah, but …' Alan had a strange look on his face; he was agitated and babbling. 'Shit,' he said, 'nobody knows that.'

Pete didn't stop there.

'Tell him about the gold chain we should have got rid of but didn't, and when we went to have those tattoos done and we bottled out.'

'All right,' Alan said at last. 'Enough. I believe you.'

Alan was blown away. I made him a cup of tea and we sat together on the sofa.

'It's real, isn't it?' he said quietly.

'Yes,' I said.

Alan was in love with another girl and we spent hours talking about their difficult relationship. I gave him advice on making it come right. One afternoon, I was looking at him and his dark eyes seemed really liquid. Suddenly his teeth looked whiter and his cheekbones more defined. He started to glow in ways only I could see. The words 'he's lovely' came into my head. He was talking to me about another girl.

Flustered, I got up and went into the kitchen to make tea. The last thing I needed was to have big emotions for somebody. I made a decision that I would never tell him how I felt.

The cottage was two miles away from Andy's farmhouse with a direct route across the fields. In the first month, he came twice and took Tanya out for a few hours. We had been in the cottage a month, when he telephoned and asked me to go and see him. I did not want to go inside the house, so we talked in the garden.

'I think we might have made a mistake splitting up,' he said. 'I'm worried about Tanya. Being apart from her does not feel right.'

'There's nothing stopping you seeing Tanya whenever you want to,' I told him, 'but I like my own space. I'm not coming back.'

A few evenings later, he telephoned.

'Someone told me Alan Salmon has been coming round,' he said.

'Yes,' I said. 'He's been helping Jed decorate.'

'I don't want scumbags like that near my daughter.'

I was shocked.

'What on earth can you have against Alan?' I asked. 'He's never done anything wrong to anybody.'

'I'm telling you I don't want him round there.' Andy's tone was threatening. 'Sort it out.'

Alan had started staying over some nights, in Shane's room. I decided not to tell him about Andy's threats, but then Andy called again.

'You're not listening to what I'm saying,' he said. 'I'm trying to do this the nice way. I don't want that guy – or any other – in the house with my daughter.'

I started lying to Andy, telling him Alan wasn't staying, but his calls got angrier. He told me how selfish I was, thinking of myself rather than what was good for Tanya. He started calling late at night and in the early hours of the morning.

'I'm going to come across the fields and cut your fucking head off,' he said.

His threats unnerved me, but I was getting braver. He was all mouth – that's what I told myself. He would not actually do anything.

Two weeks after the first call, Andy rang in the afternoon.

'He's there,' he said, 'isn't he?'

Alan was in the front room, watching TV with Shane and Tanya.

'No, he's not,' I lied. 'What's your problem?'

'Don't talk to me like that, you cunt.'

Andy's voice was ice.

'Fuck off,' I said.

It was the bravest thing I ever said to him.

'You've pushed it too far,' he said and slammed the phone down.

I called Alan into the kitchen and told him I thought Andy had lost it. Then I locked the doors and made sure the windows were closed.

'Don't tell the kids,' I said.

Fifteen minutes later, Andy was at the back door. I pushed Alan into the front room with Shane and Tanya.

'Whatever you do, don't come through or let the kids through,' I warned him.

Alan started to protest, but I was adamant.

'You will just cause more problems,' I said.

Andy kicked the back door so hard the lock broke. His face was thunder. My heart was hammering.

'What's the matter?' I asked, trying to calm him.

'You cunt,' he said.

He drew back his fist and punched me in the face. I ended up on the other side of the kitchen. Then he was straddling my body; he had a knife in his hand and he put it up against my throat.

'You've pushed it too far this time,' he hissed.

I thought: 'He's going to kill me.' I started thinking really quickly.

'You're right,' I said. I told him what he wanted to hear. 'I've probably got above myself. You know what I'm like; I say things I shouldn't.'

Tanya – the thought of her might stop him.

'Tanya's in the other room,' I said. 'You don't want to scare Tanya.'

I could feel his rage beginning to abate.

'You don't want to do this Andy,' I said. 'Imagine what Tanya would think.'

He got off me and I stood up quickly, still talking.

'Go back to the house and I'll settle the kids and come and see you,' I said. 'We can talk about it at the farmhouse.'

I walked with him to his car.

'Don't think you can fob me off,' he said. 'If you're not round within the hour, I'll be back.'

Andy got into the car, threw the knife on the floor in front of the passenger seat and drove off. I walked back into the house; my face was bruising up.

'Are you all right, Mum?' Shane was scared.

Tanya was crying. Alan was trying to comfort her. For the first time, I let myself see what Andy's violence towards me was doing to them. It tore my heart. My mind was racing. I thought that by leaving Andy, the violence would stop, but even though I was no longer living with him, he still felt he had rights on me. He would do this again. Again and again.

We could run away. We could go somewhere he would never find us. But you can't always run – deep inside I knew that. I picked up the telephone and dialled 999.

'My ex-husband has just kicked my back door down and hit me,' I informed them. 'He's threatened to kill me. He said he's coming back.'

The police arrested Andy. He denied everything, but he was charged with forced entry, actual bodily harm and threat to kill. I thought he would be kept in jail on remand, but they let him out the next day. I was terrified.

Alan's mum lived near Cambridge, so we packed up the car and the four of us went to stay in her spare room. After a few days, I discovered that although Andy had been bailed, he was not allowed within three miles of where I was – that meant he was not even allowed back to his farmhouse. It was safe for us to go home.

Back in the cottage, I kept thinking Andy was going to turn

up. He had had a string of girlfriends over the years; now the latest, Lesley, telephoned.

'Andy really doesn't want any more trouble,' she told me. 'If you let the charges go, he won't bother you any more.'

I listened to her in silence.

'We just want to get on with our life,' she said.

'I'll think about it,' I said.

A few weeks later, for the sake of Tanya and her relationship with her dad, I went to the police station. I dropped the charges but asked them to stop Andy coming near me. I did not want vengeance, I just wanted to be left alone.

When Lesley rang back, I told her what I had done.

'You better tell him, it's still on the books,' I said. 'If he even gets angry on the phone with me, I will bring the charge back.'

It was the last time I had trouble from Andy. It was over.

I carried on listening to Alan and advised him about his relationship but, increasingly, I'd find myself unable to concentrate. Instead, I would be looking at his lips and wondering what it would be like to kiss him. For the first time in my life, I lusted after somebody I couldn't have. It was a new emotion for me.

I wanted Alan for myself so the human part of me wanted to sabotage his relationship. It was a test of my morality. Alan totally trusted me and I could easily have turned his mind against his girlfriend. But if I truly cared for him, I would do everything in my power to help him win her back.

Alan had been a real friend to me. He did everything he could, without asking for anything for himself. He was a good man. That's why I offered to lend him my car.

'You need to talk to your girlfriend and be really direct and honest,' I advised him. 'Use my car and take her out somewhere special.'

The next morning, when he brought my car back, Alan let himself in through the kitchen door. I was washing up, hands in soapy suds, my whole being conscious of the fact that, the night before, he had been with another woman. I put a smile on my face.

'How did it go then?'

'Well,' Alan said, 'I've sorted things out.'

My heart sank.

'That's really good,' I said.

I could not look at him, so I continued washing teacups.

I said. 'I'm really pleased. See, it was worth the effort.'

Suddenly he was standing next to me.

'What I sorted out is I don't love her anymore.' He was grinning at me. 'Only I could be so stupid,' he said. 'All these emotions I was feeling – and you were here all the time.'

He leant over and kissed me on the lips. I still had my hands in the washing up. He stepped back.

'I shouldn't have done that,' he said.

'It's okay,' I said. 'It's more than okay.'

So we did it again.

Alan was a total contrast to Andy. For the first time in my life, a man was showing me that he loved me. The love became warmer, safer; there was a serenity I could bathe in. It was as if I had been gasping for air and suddenly the room was full of oxygen.

Alan and I used to go for walks across the fields, filled with wildflowers. We'd sit on the riverbank watching the butterflies and birds. It was a magical time.

In an intimate relationship, two people create an energy. The more you love each other when you are together, the more energy is created and it hurts to be apart. Love is a gift, the height of goodness. People don't do bad deeds when they are in love. They become more giving, more caring.

But 'in love' is conditional – it depends on the other person loving you exclusively, it depends on them not hurting you. Being in love is beautiful – and potentially destructive. Before I was psychic, I was judgmental about people who had affairs. Once I could feel people's emotions, I realized few people choose to fall in love with someone else – it causes chaos and pain and, often, they still love their partner in a gentle way. But there is no choice. Love comes from something higher than us.

For the past 12 years, my emotional food had come from my readings – they gave me a sense of worth, the feeling I was doing something useful. But now, at the height of being in love, I didn't want to do any readings. I only wanted to spend time with Alan.

A loved-up Mia was weird.

'You have a business and two kids,' Belinda used to say to me. 'Will you please talk about something other than Alan?'

When two people fall in love, it is intense because the love is not spread around. Its concentration makes it the closest thing to heaven you will experience on Earth. Anybody who has had an out-of-body experience and arrived at the end of the tunnel, feels that love and does not want to come back.

We decided to have a party – the first party I ever had. Jed hired an old ambulance and taxied people from the island. The party started in the afternoon and went on into the night with a big barbecue and a karaoke machine.

There was a wonderful atmosphere. Everyone was so happy. In between bouts of being sociable, Alan kept coming over to me, whispering in my ear and kissing me. People ended up sleeping on the floor, staggering home the next afternoon. Andy would have been horrified.

A few weeks later, Alan, Shane, Tanya and I entered a pool competition in the village pub. Walking back, there was a clear summer moon lighting our path to the cottage. Alan and Shane were walking ahead, pushing and shoving each other and generally being silly. The bond between them had grown so quickly. They genuinely enjoyed each other's company.

Tanya and I dawdled behind, talking about her plans with her best friend Virginia. The moment felt so normal – so lovely in its simplicity. Andy and I had never had a night out with the children – never had this feeling of family. It was the way it always should have been.

Shortly after, our landlord crashed his Landrover into the front of my car. I was shaken up – and I panicked. Moments before the cars collided, Alan and I had been discussing our financial crisis: to clear our debts and get our heads above water, we needed to find £1,000. A broken car was the last thing we needed.

'Are you all right?' Our landlord was solicitous.

He took a look at the car.

'I'd rather not get the insurers involved,' he said. 'Can I make you an offer?'

I nodded.

'Can I give you £1,000 for the damage?'

It was exactly the amount we needed. A week later, the landlord told us he needed the cottage for a farm labourer who was starting work. I had lived there for six months. It was time to move on.

The new cottage was again in the middle of nowhere. It had three bedrooms and a huge garage. Alan immediately filled the garage with tatty, old wooden furniture, which he started to restore and sell. Shane was always in there, talking to him. Alan had so much time for Shane.

Within two weeks of moving into our new cottage, my friend Janet telephoned in tears. Her 16-year-old son, Luke, was causing problems at home. She did not know what to do. Luke and Shane had been close friends since they were babies; the solution seemed obvious.

'Why doesn't Luke come and stay with us for a couple of weeks?' I suggested. 'That will give you some space.'

'Are you sure?'

'Kids always behave better when they are away from their parents,' I said.

The house had three bedrooms, so we moved Luke into the biggest room, with Shane. He settled in really quickly. Then, a week later, Jed's son, Steven, came to see me. He told me a long elaborate story about why he couldn't stay with his parents. It did not make a lot of sense, but he obviously wanted to stay with me, so I invited him to live with us for a little while until he sorted himself out.

I ended up buying bunk beds for the boys. With six of us, the house was chaotic and overcrowded, but the children loved it. They were constantly joking and messing about. There was always raucous laughter coming from the top of the house.

Shane had no memory of his real dad and he said he wanted to meet him. I finally located Mick in Dublin and, after they had spoken on the telephone, Mick came over to meet him. Mick had completely cleaned up his act and was in a good relationship. Shane went to visit Mick several times in Dublin and they grew close. It was lovely for both of them. Shane was very proud of his dad.

Gradually, the intense feelings between Alan and I settled into something more compatible with daily living. We were finally able to see something other than each other and we opened back up. Having Luke and Steven gave us a chance to be helpful. We both enjoyed that. Alan was so good with the children, so enduringly patient, honest and real.

He found a skinny stray cat in the street and brought it home. Two months later it produced four kittens. We bought a playpen from a car boot sale and the kittens lived in that.

The house was a mess of litter trays, cat food, kittens and kids.

I got expert at feeding them all cheaply. Each week I bought piles of cheap bread, potatoes and cheese; also cardboard boxes of broken biscuits from the pound store. One afternoon, a biker couple who lived nearby asked if they could park their caravan outside our house. They only used it to go to festivals a couple of times a year and knew we had a house full of teenagers; they said that we could use it.

The boys were ecstatic. The extension cable from the front room stretched to the caravan, which they filled with a stereo, speakers and candles. They had their own club-house and teenagers turned up from all over. There would be 20 or more of them squeezed in there. All the time they were there, I reasoned, at least they weren't getting into trouble.

At night, one by one the boys would come in to say good-night to us. Shane always kissed me and said, 'I love you.'

One morning, I got up before anyone else and saw something moving in the caravan. The boys always slept in their bunks upstairs, so I went out to investigate. It was a small, thin, white-looking boy. He had obviously been sleeping in the caravan and he looked terrified. He was wrapped in blankets I recognized from the bedroom.

'Shane said I could stay the night.'

'It's all right, love,' I told him. 'Come in and have a cup of tea.'

He looked so young. I wondered if his parents knew he'd been out all night. I took him into the kitchen and while

Alan made him tea and toast, I went to the boys' bedroom and woke them up.

'Who's the kid in the caravan?'

'Paul.'

He was 16 and his mum had thrown him out. He was starving so they bought him a burger and brought him back to the caravan. He had been staying there for nearly a week.

'Why didn't you tell me?'

'There's four of us,' Steven said. 'We didn't think you'd want any more.'

They all looked at me.

I went back to the kitchen where Paul was quietly eating toast. He looked so scared. I sat at the kitchen table and asked him to tell me what happened. He'd been in trouble with the police over a minor theft and his mum, struggling on her own with three other children, said she couldn't cope with him and told him to leave.

A mother had thrown her child onto the street – it was beyond my comprehension. Alan was standing against the kitchen units, listening. I looked at him and he nodded at me.

When Paul went upstairs, I said to Alan, 'What does one more matter?'

Alan agreed. 'We can't throw him out.'

We found a carrier bag full of grimy clothes in the caravan and put them in the washing machine. The boys sorted him out something to wear and we all had a big breakfast. Over the next few days, Alan and I found another set of bunk beds and then the bedroom was filled with four boys between the ages of 16 and 17. It was mayhem.

All the troubled lads in the area came to our house. They were always in the kitchen with me, telling me their problems. I used to find them in the morning, sleeping in the caravan, on the bedroom floor or doubling up in the bunk beds.

Luke, Steven and Paul all had social workers who advised us not to have them in the house. That got my back up.

'I think I'll decide that for myself,' I said.

They were known as petty crooks and thieves, but no one ever took anything from our house.

15

The telephone rang constantly – either with clients, my family or the children's mates. I trained the boys to take messages from my clients. When they came, I banned the boys to the caravan – unless my clients were the girls from the local hairdressers. Then the testosterone-loaded lads could not be confined, but were suddenly transformed into courteous tea-makers.

One evening, the seven of us were watching TV with the obligatory box of broken biscuits and bottle of cheap coke, when the telephone rang. Steven jumped up and went to the hall. It was 10.15 p.m. A few moments later, he put his head round the door.

'You've got a ghost.'

'What – on the phone?'

We all burst out laughing and Steven put his hand over the phone.

'No, someone is talking about having a ghost in their flat.'

A man told me, his voice shaking, that the TV remote control had been thrown across the room and the TV was switching channels by itself. Also, a large armchair had moved and the microwave was going round without anyone touching it.

'Can you come now?'

'Are you sure this can't wait until the morning?'

He sounded desperate. 'I can pick you up – I'll come now with my mate.'

As Alan and I put on our coats and shoes, the boys serenaded us with a chorus of 'Ghostbusters'. Outside, in a two-door Fiat hatchback, sat two of the biggest men I have ever seen. Their heads were shaven and their arms were covered with tattoos. The lane was dark and isolated, but we weren't worried getting into the car – they looked like two terrified children.

In the car, the men gabbled, 'I've never seen anything like this before … a mate had your number … I didn't believe in ghosts …'

The front room of the maisonette was crowded with neighbours, feeding each other's fear. In the kitchen, a young woman sat alone at a table. I opened up and psychically scanned the flat. I could feel chaos but I wasn't sure what was going on. All I knew for sure was that it did not feel bad.

I went to sit with the young girl. She was so scared. She told me she had a three-year-old son and this was their flat. For the last two months, her son had been talking about a little girl playing with him. She had assumed he had an imaginary friend.

'But two nights ago I woke up to hear a child crying. I thought it was my son but when I went into his bedroom, he was asleep. I could still clearly hear a child crying. I was at the top of the stairs and, as I looked down, I saw a little girl sitting on the bottom step.

'I thought she had wandered in and got lost. I walked down the stairs and as I leant over to put my hand on her shoulder, she disappeared. At that moment,' she added, 'my nose suddenly poured with blood.'

I asked if I could walk around the flat. The girl's son had been sent to stay elsewhere, but as I walked into his bedroom, I saw a little girl of about four years old.

She had fair hair and was wearing a white calico dress. She was kneeling over the toy box. She was slightly shimmery, as if she was being lit from the inside, but she was so clear to me.

'Can you see her?' I asked Alan.

'No,' he said, 'see what?'

I walked towards the little girl and knelt beside her. She turned round and looked at me.

'Hello darling,' I said.

She smiled. I had the feeling nobody had spoken to her in a long time. But, as with all the spirits I'd seen, although she was lost, she was clearly not afraid. I saw Eric in my mind. I saw him standing behind the girl and, next to him, a hazy ball of light was forming. Noises from downstairs broke through the stillness of the room and the light faded.

I relaxed and opened up again; behind the little girl, the light started to build and get brighter. Then I heard noises and I lost it again. I started to feel frustrated. This could go on all night. I told Alan what was going on and, as I did, an idea started to form.

'I don't know,' I told him, 'but I think I might be able to take her with us.'

I bent down and said to the little girl, 'Stay with me. I want to take you home.'

She nodded. I wasn't sure if it would work, but I had a feeling she was going to stick with me. We went downstairs to the woman in the kitchen.

'Did you find anything?'

The little girl was still beside me, happily skipping around.

'Yes,' I said, 'and it's gone. It was just a little girl.'

She went in to the front room and told the assembled neighbours, 'She's got rid of it.'

I walked in behind her and the little girl skipped around the room, looking up at people. It amused me to think how freaked out they'd be if they realized a spirit was walking among them.

'Does she always work so quickly?' a big, burly guy asked Alan.

Alan looked at me. 'She's good at sorting things out.'

After we left the house, I took a deep breath. Spirits can become stuck to a place; I still did not know whether the little girl would come with me. I took three steps outside the front door and looked to my side. She was walking beside me.

I felt protective towards her. I was responsible for a young child – but one I couldn't grab hold of. She got into the back of the car with me and determinedly climbed onto my lap. I could not feel her weight.

As we were driving, she leaned forward and tickled the back of the driver's neck. I watched him scratch the place where her fingers touched him.

He said, 'I'm so glad you managed to sort it out. Anything like that scares the shit out of me. I'd rather have a raving lunatic on my hands than a ghost.'

I told Alan not to tell the teenagers that I'd brought the little girl home. As we sat on the sofa, chatting with the boys, she stayed close, curiously observing everything and, from time to time, touching Alan's cheek.

Eventually, the teenagers went to bed.

'Is she touching my face?' Alan asked. 'I can feel something cold on my cheek.'

I was delighted. 'Yes, yes she is.'

It was the first time Alan had direct contact with a spirit.

Usually I see Eric in my head or see him peripherally, but this night he was standing in the room, looking at me. He didn't say anything, but I knew that he meant: 'Get on with it.' It was a delight to watch the girl and have her in the room – it was so magical. I wanted the feeling to last but I took one final look at her, closed my eyes, concentrated and opened up.

When I opened my eyes again, the light was there. It grew really strong; a beautiful, rich, yellow light. I saw a shadowy figure deep inside it, getting closer and more solid. Eventually, I could see a woman standing there. She knelt down and held her arms out to the little girl and she ran to her. The woman wrapped her arms around her daughter and they both sank back into the light.

Tears were streaming down my face. Eric smiled gently at me.

'Are you all right?' Alan asked. 'What happened? Why is the room so warm?'

The archway of light was still shining brightly.

'Are you crying because you are sad,' Alan asked, 'or because you are happy?'

'Happy,' I said.

Two weeks later, I received a telephone call from the woman who lived in the flat next door to the one that housed the little girl.

'It's got much worse since you were here,' she told me. 'One neighbour was pinned against the wall. Five of us have seen the spirit of a man. It is well out of control.'

I went back with Alan. This time, when I walked into the flats, the feeling I got was decidedly bad. I felt anger in the air. I knew a spirit was there, but I could not locate it.

'None of this was happening before you came,' one woman accused.

What had I done? I did not understand. There was a roomful of people, all wanting me to sort it out, and I didn't have a clue what to do. Previously, I'd seen a ghost and Eric would step in. But this time, there was no ghost – and no Eric. I needed to go somewhere quiet to talk to him. I excused myself for an hour and went home.

'What am I doing wrong? I can feel something, but I can't see it. What's going on?'

'It's the father of the little girl,' Eric said. 'He killed himself and his daughter.'

I sensed then that her father had told her to stay with him. She was just doing what she was told.

'Leave it to me,' Eric said. 'The process has already started.'

A month later, the local press telephoned and asked if I knew of any hauntings in the area. I called the young woman, but she refused to talk to them. She was terrified what people might think of her; she just wanted to go back to normal. That's why, when these experiences happen to people, they end up isolated, feeling they are the only ones.

The bikers who had so kindly lent us their caravan invited Alan and I to a party at their cottage. When we arrived there were 30 bikes outside. Inside were hard-looking men in leather jackets, torn t-shirts and tattoos. Hell's Angels they might be, but they were a lovely bunch and we all got pleasantly drunk in the front room.

Out of the corner of my eye, on a side table, I saw two black candles burning. Between them was a package wrapped in deep purple silk.

'What's that?' I asked.

'Big Dave's tarot cards.'

I leant over to pick them up.

'Don't touch the cards,' a man said.

He told me the cards had a curse on them; if anyone but Big Dave touched them, then bad luck would befall them. I looked at the men around me, expecting them to laugh, but no one did.

'You're serious?'

'Dead right, I'm serious.'

'I wouldn't touch them,' another biker said.

Curses and bad luck – what a load of rubbish. I felt indignant.

'Okay,' I said, 'we'll see about that.'

I leant over, picked up the silk-clad package and started shuffling the cards. The room went quiet. I was probably more buoyed-up by alcohol than spirituality, otherwise I would not have been so quick to offend.

Suddenly Big Dave was in front of me.

'What are you doing?' he growled.

Alan sunk deeper into the couch. No one knew what I did for a living.

'I thought I'd give you a tarot reading,' I said.

'Nobody can use those cards but me,' Dave said. 'They don't work for anybody else.'

I carried on shuffling.

'Humour me,' I said.

Dave sat opposite me.

'Go on then.'

I had never picked up Tarot cards in my life before. I didn't have a clue what anything meant. I laid seven cards in a row and looked at them. I was totally confused. I looked at the cards for a long time. I could hear sniggers.

I looked up at Big Dave. He was smirking. He looked unfriendly. I smiled and locked with his eyes. I looked back at the cards, but I was visualizing his eyes – they told me everything I needed to know.

I started doing a reading. I pretended I was using the cards to get the information. I told him about a pedal breaking on his bike and lots of little things that had been happening the previous week.

I finished it off with, 'Be careful who you tread on for they will come back to tread on you.'

I'd made the line up off the top of my head to get myself out of a situation, but everyone in the room nodded sagely at me.

'You're good,' one of them said. 'Have you done this sort of thing before?'

Alan said, 'She does it for a living, actually.'

Everyone laughed. The ice was broken. It wasn't until the next morning I realized how close I came to aggravating 30 Hell's Angels.

'Don't show off again,' Alan said.

I got a call from a pub on a quay. It was an old smugglers' inn. The landlord explained he'd seen chairs balanced on tables and ashtrays piled in unusual shapes. Belinda was showing more and more interest in my work so, this time, I took her along too.

We left Alan chatting in the bar with the landlord, while we wandered the warren of winding corridors, stairs and rooms. At the very top of the pub, we found two attic rooms. There, in an old armchair, was a young boy in an old-fashioned waistcoat and half-trousers. His feet were bare.

He had one leg hooked casually over the arm of the chair and he was looking directly at me. He was so clear, I was convinced Belinda could see him. I didn't want to put pictures in her mind, so I was deliberately casual.

'That chair in there,' I said, 'is it the same as the one at your parents' house?'

Breathless from the climb, Belinda stood in the doorway beside me. Then she froze.

'Oh my God, there's something sitting in the chair, isn't there?'

'Yes.' I was excited for her. This was what she had come to see.

'Describe it to me.'

'I can see a small shimmering figure. It's a young boy.'

Belinda turned and started running down the stairs.

'Come on,' she said.

'What are you doing? Where are you going?'

'For fuck's sake, Mia. It's a ghost.'

'Of course it's a ghost.'

She reached the bottom of the first flight of stairs.

'Are you coming?'

'No,' I said. 'I'm going to stop and have a chat.'

The boy was about 13 years old and very skinny. I tried to talk to him – sometimes I hear a ghost's voice in my head, but not with this boy. Eric came, the light built into an archway and the boy went through it. As with the little girl, sending a child over felt like a job well done.

When I came back down into the bar, Belinda was on her second double vodka.

'It was just a little boy,' I said.

'No,' Belinda said. 'It was a ghost.'

We'd had many discussions about the paranormal and Belinda had been so up for seeing a ghost. But when she was confronted with the reality she lost her nerve. I defy anyone to see a ghost and not be changed. It was a long time before Belinda came ghostbusting again.

Shortly after, I received a telephone call from a man called John Nurden. He had his own public relations company and had seen a piece about me in the local newspaper.

'You'll never believe this,' he said, 'they're building a new ghost ride at the Dreamland amusement park, but the resident engineer says the workmen are refusing to work at night because they have seen the ghost of a young woman in the tunnel.'

I could see the headline: 'Psychic Called In To Sort Out Ghost Train's Ghost.' I agreed to go on the condition that no press turned up. I was determined not to be part of a publicity stunt.

It was out of season and Dreamland was closed for repairs and repainting. I talked to the workmen. I still thought it was a hoax but they were adamant they had seen a ghost.

'There were these strange whispering noises and cold,' they told me. 'It was like being in a fridge.'

The tunnel was softly lit with work lights and, as I walked along, I saw her leaning up against the wall. She was about 20, wearing long skirts and a brown top buttoned to the wrists and neck. Her feet were bare. I was shocked. I really had not expected to see her.

Alan was with me and, as usual, I checked whether he could see anything.

'No,' he said, 'but I can feel the temperature has dropped.'

I walked closer to the woman. She looked as if she had been crying. I looked in her eyes and knew she wanted me to help her. She was the first spirit I had seen that had been distressed.

I closed my eyes and opened up; there was a slight shimmer of the yellow arch, but she didn't move towards it. She just stood there looking at me, with pain in her face. The doorway became more solid but still she did not go through it.

'This is new to me; this isn't meant to happen,' I told Alan. 'Every other time, the ghost has gone towards the light.'

'She probably wants to tell you something,' Alan said.

'Do you want to talk to me?' I asked. 'What is it?'

Her eyes were flickering with uncertainty, but she did not speak. Then, suddenly, my head was filled with pictures. I saw her standing by a Victorian fairground ride with her father. He was a Romany gipsy; he'd set up the original fairground. I saw her put a shawl around her shoulders and walk through the fairground. She went under an underpass; there I saw an attack. A man twice her size raped and killed her.

Then I saw a newspaper headline: 'Prostitute Murdered.' I knew then what was troubling her so deeply. She was not a prostitute; to be branded as such in the nineteenth century was so distressing it stopped her going over.

The pictures stopped. I looked at her again.

'I'll tell them you weren't a prostitute,' I promised. 'I'll tell the truth – you can go over now.'

I saw Eric by the doorway and she went slowly towards it. Just before she went through, she stopped and looked at me again.

'Who are you going to tell?' Alan asked.

'I don't know,' I said, 'but I made a promise.'

We walked back through the tunnel and the workmen were waiting.

'Did you see her?'

'Yes,' I said, 'she's gone now.'

I had been promised the press would not be there, but as we walked into the sunlight, someone stuck a microphone in my face and fired questions at me. A flashbulb went off. I was annoyed, but then I thought: 'I can set the record straight.'

'There is a story that, a hundred years ago, a prostitute was raped and killed in one of the tunnels under the park,' I said. 'The truth is she invited a local labourer to the fair for an evening out, but when she rejected his advances he flew into a rage, raped and killed her. She wants it known she was a good girl.'

One of my regular clients, Vera, rang.

'I wondered if you could help us raise funds for the campaign against live exports,' she said. 'Maybe you could give a clairvoyant show.'

I had seen television footage of the cattle trucks on the docks, crammed with calves so that veal-lovers across the Channel could have their meat fresher. These baby animals were being transported without sufficient food and water. I had heard them crying and had been horrified. It was so wrong.

'They are going to die anyway, so no one cares,' Vera said.

I had never done a public demonstration of clairvoyance before, but Vera said it would be just a small gathering of people. I wanted to help the campaign and I agreed to do it in three weeks time.

A week later, I saw a poster in the High Street advertizing me. I telephoned Vera.

'I thought it was just going to be a small audience,' I said.

Vera was reassuring. 'No matter how much you advertize, you only ever get about twenty or thirty people,' she said.

On the night of the fund-raising demonstration, Alan and I turned up at the hall 45 minutes before I was due to go on. People were queuing outside and the hall was already filling up. I went to find Vera, fully expecting her to tell me there was something else going on as well.

'Isn't it wonderful, dear?' she said. 'They're all here for you and we've got ages to go yet.'

I thought I was just going to talk to a few people. I peered through the curtain – there was a stage – *a stage* – and staff were bringing out more and more chairs and arranging them in tightly-packed rows. I was horrified.

What would I do? I would not be close enough to see people's eyes, so I would need to be very relaxed to see their auras. But would I be able to be relaxed in that setting? I was in total panic. Maybe I could clutch my chest and pretend to pass out. Or perhaps I could offer everyone a free reading at a later date.

Alan and I were taken to a makeshift dressing room. It had a small plastic chair and a pink plastic mirror. I was shaking all over. I'd only ever done clairvoyance from a calm, floaty place. How on earth was I going to relax in front of so many people?

I rummaged around at the bottom of my bag and found eyeliner and mascara, also a broken lipstick which doubled up as lip colour and rouge. I did not have a hairbrush, so I went for the tousled look.

Vera came in.

'All right, dear?'

'How long am I meant to be doing it for?'

'I thought we'd do an hour, have an interval, then do another hour,' she said.

I looked at her beautiful blouse and suit. I suddenly thought of my clothes – I was wearing black trousers and a blue shirt I'd bought in the market. Most of the audience were better dressed than I was.

'You've got seven minutes before you go on. Try to calm down before going on stage,' Alan said.

'You go on the bloody stage,' I hissed at him.

I tried to close my eyes, relax and see if I could open up, but all I could hear was the noise of the hall – filled with people and laughter. Oh God, I could not open up. I left the room quickly and saw a little door in the passageway. The broom cupboard. I went in and shut the door. It was black in there. I leant back against the wall. The sound of the audience was muffled.

'Eric,' I called. 'Eric.'

'Relax,' he said. 'Relax and open up.'

'I can't do it. Please help me. I'll never say yes to anything like this again. Please get me out of it.'

'Open up,' he said again.

I started to float and immediately I was in Eric's place. We were sitting on logs either side of the fire; there were trees around us.

'Have faith,' Eric said.

'I trust you, Eric,' I said. 'It's me I don't trust.'

But, looking at the fire, I was starting to feel calmer.

'Just have faith,' he said.

There was a knock at the door.

'It's time,' Alan said.

The hall was packed: 150 people – and me.

Vera introduced me and then passed me the microphone. I had never used one before. Clutching it to me, I walked up the three wooden steps to the stage and looked out at the big sea of faces.

I stood there unable to say anything; the seconds felt like years.

'Thank you,' I said at last. 'My name's Mia Dolan and I've been working as a psychic for fifteen years.'

As I spoke, I frantically searched the audience for someone I could go into.

'I'd like to thank you all for coming along. Please bear with me, as I've never worked with such a large number of people.'

I looked over to the left of the audience because I saw someone tall standing there. It was Pete. He was as real and as solid as anyone there. Pete was pointing at the man in front of him and grinning at me. I looked at the man and I could see the colours of his aura. I was drawn in.

'You've had trouble starting your car in the last couple of days,' I told him.

'I had to jump start it to get here tonight,' he replied.

The audience laughed. It was a great ice-breaker. I looked

at Pete – having him there was a massive relief. Maybe I could do this after all.

As I relaxed, I got more and more images – and more feedback and laughter. I saw people's auras glowing and went towards them. The more I did, the calmer I became. I was in the zone now; no worries, no nerves.

The next thing I knew, Vera was standing in front of the stage, letting me know I had run ten minutes over the hour. When I went back on for the second half, I was relaxed. Eric was there; Pete too, moving around the room.

'I'm afraid I've got to stop now,' I told the audience. 'I'd like to thank you so much for coming along to help raise money for such a worthwhile cause. I hope you found this evening interesting and, if anyone would like to ask me any questions, I'll be available after the show.'

It was a throwaway comment. I was on a high, flooded with relief and a feeling of well-being.

'I think you made quite an impact, dear,' Vera said as she bustled into the storage/changing room. 'There's a few people wanting to have a word with you.'

The queue stretched right round the hall. I was exhausted, but it was an honour that all these people wanted to talk to me, so I sat on the edge of the stage and, one by one, I listened to their worries and problems and gave them my advice. I did as much reassuring as I did psychic work. Alan and I did not get away until after midnight.

16

Luke, Steven and Paul's social workers came to the cottage. They told us that a new one-year course, 'Breaking The Cycle' was starting. It was aimed at teenagers who had been in trouble with the police or had problems at school. Luke, Steven and Paul were all entitled to go on it – and although they had never broken the law, Shane and Tanya were granted places too.

We moved again. This time there was more space and an enormous outbuilding which Alan immediately filled with old furniture, waxes and stains. Life settled into a routine then; with the five teenagers on the course, busy doing outward-bound exercises and learning music production, I did more and more readings.

A woman rang me and told me her daughter was being haunted by a poltergeist.

'Objects are being thrown around and electrical things go mad when my daughter is in the room. We had a priest in,' she added. 'He did an exorcism, but it didn't work. So we took her to the head office of the Spiritualist Society, but that didn't work either. We don't know what to do.'

In the lounge, the girl's aura was exploding like a volcano. Straightaway, I knew what was going on. Everyone else had been trying to exorcise a ghost or entity, that's why they were unsuccessful. This girl wasn't being haunted – she was having a massive spiritual awakening, similar to the one that I went through.

'Weird stuff's been happening to me,' she said. 'I was in the kitchen and cups moved. Yesterday a knife came across the counter in front of me. The television turns itself off or changes channels when I'm around.'

I sat by her on the couch and held her hand. She was crying. I explained to her that it was her own energy that was making these things happen. I told her about when it first started happening to me, but it did not comfort her.

'I don't like it,' she said. 'I'm not like that.'

I did not know what to do to help her, but words came into my head, so I said, 'What I'm going to do is close you down. For the next three or four days, you'll feel extremely tired and prob-ably sleep a lot. That will wear off, then you'll be fine and all this will stop.'

I did not know why I said it – or how to shut her down. As soon as I got home, I opened up. Eric was there straightaway. I expected him to be cross.

'I'm really sorry, Eric. I said I'd do all that stuff and I should-n't have. Can you help me help her?'

I paused for breath. He was smiling at me.

'You were meant to say that,' he said. 'We are closing her down.'

Five days later, the girl's mother telephoned.

'I just wanted to let you know that you were right,' she said. 'She stayed off school and slept for three days and now it's all stopped. We feel like we've got our daughter back.'

I never set out to be a rescue worker – or a 'ghostbuster', as my family say to tease me – but word got around. One evening, an employee from the local cottage hospital telephoned me.

'We've had some really heavy stuff going on here,' she told me. 'The staff are scared to do the night shift. It's been a joke in the hospital for years that strange things go on, but over the last few weeks there really is something happening. One nurse was pushed onto a trolley bed and then spun across the room. A male nurse was thrown across the room and pinned up against the wall. Can you help?'

Management said we could go in when the patients were asleep. As soon as Alan and I arrived, I saw the spirit of a little old man holding a cloth cap in his hand. He walked with us along the corridor to the nurse's rest room.

As the nurse told her story, the old man walked around the room. He would be easy to deal with, I thought. I listened to the events that had scared the staff, but I was convinced I could sort it out in minutes.

Most of the activity was centred around one treatment room, so I decided that this would be the best place to send the man over. I found the room easily; the energy coming from it was like electricity.

The room was furnished with two chairs and an examination couch. There were healthcare posters on the walls. Alone in there with Alan, I assured him the ghost was small and amiable.

'And he throws nurses about?' Alan was uncertain.

'Physical energy is irrelevant in the spirit world,' I said, with authority.

I did not centre or ground myself – I was so confident – I just sat on one of the chairs and opened up. Bang. My head exploded with screams and cries and moans. It was an awful nightmarish sound. I saw distorted faces, coming at me from every direction. I could not even close my eyes to get away – they were inside my head.

I had never come across anything like this before. I was terrified I would go under – it was so powerful – I felt I was going to black out, lose my mind.

I called for Eric and I heard his voice through the din.

'Stay with it, hold it.'

It was like holding onto the sides of an aircraft that's been ripped open in the sky. A force was trying to drag me out. Faces, voices, noises; there was a whack of light in the middle of the room. It filled the room with brightness, then contracted back to a ball. Then it was gone.

All was still. It was an enormous relief to see the chairs and the wall – everything looked normal. Alan was in front of me, holding my hands.

'You've been shaking violently and moaning,' he said. 'You really scared me. Are you all right?'

'It felt like fifty ghosts all trying to get in my head at the same time,' I said. 'I've been lost in it. I have no idea what my body's been doing.'

Usually, all I had to do was see a ghost, feel it, concentrate and let Eric take it over. I had been getting more and more confident, but my encounter with the spirits at the hospital frightened me. I had opened up and, whatever it was, had jumped into me and invaded my mind.

As soon as I got home, I called for Eric, 'What happened? There were so many spirits – so many faces and noises and voices.'

'It wasn't spirit,' Eric said. 'It was leftover energy.'

'Left over from what?'

'So many people dying in confusion and agitation and fear. It became an energy of its own.'

'The more emotional pain and turmoil the person dies in, the stronger the trace?'

'Yes.'

'What about the faces and the screaming and moaning?'

'Like the little boy you saw fall down the stairs,' Eric explained, 'they weren't there, it was just an imprint.'

Despite Eric's words, I still felt wary. I thought about giving up rescuing spirits. I was afraid for my sanity. I did not want to be overwhelmed again.

Ten days later, I received a phone call from the same nurse.

'We think it's starting up again,' she said. 'We're really worried. Can you come back?'

Oh God. I was filled with dread. I did not want to go but I knew I had to. I did not have a choice. I was sick with fear.

Alan and I went back the same night and I went straight to the room. Instead of opening up casually as I had the time before, I centred myself as carefully as I could. When I felt calm and strong inside, I visualized white light all around me, then I opened very slightly and asked Eric to come.

Eric was crystal clear in my mind. He was standing with both hands on his stick, looking at me.

'So now you do it properly,' he said.

'Yes,' I was distracted, impatient to get on with it and get out of there. 'Will you help me this time? Can we do it together?'

'You have already done what you came for.'

'We've got to get rid of something else.'

'No,' Eric said, 'you came back to learn a lesson.'

'What do you mean?'

'You will never know until you open up what you are going to find. Never become over-confident or blasé.'

'So you brought me back,' I said. I realized that it must have been Eric who scared the nurses.

'You made things happen?'

'Just a little,' he said.

Leaving the hospital that night, I felt such relief. Eric had made me go back and face my fear and see if I would do it properly. I felt I'd passed a test at the second attempt. I took Eric's words on board: 'Never think you know everything. Always stay solid and grounded.'

Sky Television contacted John Nurden. They were looking for a psychic for a show and he gave them my number.

'John told us you believe everyone has the ability to use their sixth sense in some way – is that right?' the researcher asked.

'Yes, I totally believe that.'

'Would you be prepared to come on television and talk about it?'

It sounded an interesting experience.

'Yes, I'd love to.'

Towards the end of the conversation, the researcher asked me, 'You have done live television before, haven't you?'

'Yes, of course,' I lied.

How hard could live television be?

Belinda drove me to London. I was not nervous at all – not even when I saw how big the security gates and buildings were. It was fun having someone style my hair and apply my make-up. We sat in the Green Room with a terrified-looking man from the homeless charity, Shelter. He was clutching his notes while I chain-smoked nonchalantly.

'I can't believe how relaxed you are,' Belinda said for the tenth time. 'If I was going on television, I'd be really nervous.'

'It's just a big camera,' I said confidently.

Ten minutes before I was due to go on, the assistant put her head around the door.

'Everything all right? Anyone need anything?'

'Can I just ask you' – Belinda said, 'how many people will be watching?'

'Fifty million.'

'What?' I said. 'Don't be ridiculous. I don't know anyone with Sky – and, anyway, there's not that many people in Britain.'

'This programme is broadcast all around the world,' the assistant said.

Belinda had her hand over her mouth; she was looking at me with big scared eyes.

'Oh my God.'

I was suddenly aware that my heart was banging in my chest. The man from Shelter was stone grey and beads of sweat started to appear on his forehead. This was information we did not need to have.

I went to the toilets and ran my wrists under the cold tap. It was the only thing I could think of doing; I vaguely remembered hearing somewhere that it could calm you down.

As the assistant escorted me onto the set, she said again, 'You have done live TV before, haven't you?'

There was no point in causing problems now.

'Yes,' I said.

Two presenters were seated on a couch in front of cameras. I was fascinated; the cameras were remote-controlled. Behind a glass partition, a group of people were watching us. Countdown: '5 ... 4 ... 3 ... 2 ... 1...'

'We've got Mia Dolan with us. She is a psychic from Kent and she has a theory that everyone has an ability to use their sixth sense. So,' the male presenter said, turning to me, 'can we all link in with our paranormal powers, Mia?'

I was on home ground.

'Everyone has a sixth sense. We're all born with it. Most of us lose it because of religious doctrine or society's rules.'

'So somebody who does not believe in anything like this could still be psychic?'

'Yes,' I agreed, 'but obviously to different degrees. It's a case of varying abilities.'

'Don't you think people like you prey on the vulnerable?' The female presenter was looking at me coldly. 'This business of ghosts – isn't it hype to make people like you more interesting?'

I felt a flash of anger – she was insulting me – but the question was fair.

'I can understand people not believing in it,' I said, 'and I'm not saying anyone should. I'm only telling you what I believe through the experiences I have had. I went from being an atheist to where I am today.'

'Let's face it Mia, isn't it mostly about people who want to find out who their next boyfriend is going to be or when they're going to be rich?' the woman continued. 'They cross your palm with silver like they do with gipsies.'

I was settling into it now. We were having a debate.

'Of course some people come to see me about relationships and money issues, but it's not as flippant as you've made it sound. When people are going through a relationship breakdown, their lives can be devastated. The most important thing I do is try to let people see that life doesn't just consist of where they are at this minute. Most people are just interested in how they feel right now, but when you are using your sixth sense, you realize that your life is yesterday, today and tomorrow.'

The interview went on for 15 minutes. As the male presenter wrapped it up and thanked me for coming, he said, 'I must apologize for my colleague. I think she got out of the wrong side of the bed this morning.'

The woman was shuffling papers and glaring at me.

'Well done,' the producer said. 'You managed to tackle that very well. You've obviously done this before.'

My first experience of live TV.

The funniest call I ever got was from John Nurden, who was now acting for me as my unofficial agent.

'I've just turned down a presenting job for you,' he said. 'It would have given you your own show in Scandinavia.'

'Don't you think you could have talked to me about it first?' – I was incensed.

John laughed, 'I knew you wouldn't want it.'

'How could you know?'

'They wanted the psychic presenter to go topless.'

Two months later, Radio Kent asked if I would do a phone-in session on the air.

'What do you mean by phone-in?' I asked.

'People call up the radio station and you can give them little readings on the phone.'

I was very much against the psychic phone lines in the papers – charging people you have never met for a reading.

'I'll happily come in and answer questions, but I can't promise I can do readings from phone calls,' I told the researcher.

She said, 'Let's see how it goes.'

From the moment I got to the radio station, I loved it. I could be scruffy and wear no make-up – all they wanted was my voice. I put the headphones on. There was a microphone in front of me.

The first two questions were about minor phenomena that people had experienced. The third caller asked, 'Can you tell me anything about myself?'

I was just about to say, 'I don't do readings on the phone,' when I saw a drain in my head. It was in the road, covered by slats. I could see the woman was upset.

'I'll just tell you what I've got. I see you being upset about a drain or a drain cover.'

The woman burst out laughing.

'I didn't expect you to say that,' she said. 'A few days ago I tripped on a drain and broke my leg.'

After that the phone lines were jammed. So many people called. From that, I found I could know snippets about people I couldn't see. At the end of the show, I was asked if I would be willing to go on the show once a fortnight. So, for the next few months, I had a regular slot on local radio.

I also booked and organized a small tour of local theatres. We had a big green estate car we called 'the Bus'. We filled the back with cushions from the front room and that way it could transport the seven of us.

One show was at Herne Bay, on the coast. The children, Alan and I arrived three hours before the show was due to start.

'How many tickets have you sold for this evening?' I asked the woman at the kiosk.

'None,' she said.

I couldn't understand it. Most nights I was playing to audiences of 60–100 people. It took time to work out that no posters had been put up and the local paper had not been notified. There was not even a poster outside the theatre. Nobody knew the show was on.

We went outside. We were skint and now we would not even cover the costs of renting the theatre.

'This is ridiculous,' I said. 'We'll have to cancel.'

'Have you got any flyers?' Steven asked.

We rummaged in the car and found a box of flyers which the teenagers distributed along the high street, at the supermarket and in the market area. They harassed and cajoled the entire town so, when the curtain went up that night, the auditorium was three-quarters full.

John Nurden offered to arrange and publicize a show for me. The idea of someone else doing all the arrangements, leaving me free to just turn up on the night, appealed hugely. I didn't even go and see the theatre before the night. I left it all to John.

The Hazlet Theatre in Maidstone was a shock. Lighting engineers, sound boxes, stalls. Fifteen minutes before I was due to go on stage, I looked out between the velvet curtains and I saw 600 people, all waiting to be entertained. I had no script, nothing prepared.

I went back to the dressing room – it had lights around the mirror. Everything about the place screamed: proper theatre. What on earth was I doing there? What was I going to do?

'I've sorted out a great entrance for you,' John said backstage. Then he gave me instructions. 'When you come on the stage, I want you to walk to the centre and then down to the front.' As I started to walk up the steps onto the stage, I heard the sounds of 'Close Encounters of the Third Kind' – the sound the mother ship made when it communicated with Earth. Smoke filled the room and blue spotlights swirled everywhere. I froze.

'Go to the centre of the stage,' John whispered and prodded me in the back.

Cringing with embarrassment, I walked across the stage. When the applause died down, I said into the microphone, 'That was an amazing introduction, but let's get back down to Earth, shall we? House lights please.'

The lighting engineer turned the lights on the audience. I was shaking. I went towards a man.

'Have you been having trouble with a phone?' I asked him.

He looked at me.

'No.'

'That's strange, I got a strong irritation about a telephone,' I said. 'Oh well, never mind.'

I heard a mobile phone ring loudly.

'I'm really sorry,' the man said.

He started hitting his pocket to turn his mobile off.

We were the only people in that room who knew the situation wasn't contrived. A few people laughed. It broke the ice – and gave me confidence. I relaxed and allowed myself to float in the zone and the rest of the show passed quickly and easily.

'You said you could work from photographs,' John said one day. 'Do you think you could do it for a celebrity?'

'If I've got a good enough photo of their eyes I should be able to,' I said. 'Why?'

'We've just heard that Robbie Williams is leaving Take That. If I get you some photos of him, do you think you can predict his future?'

I said, 'I'll have a go.'

Robbie looked arrogant in his Take That pose but, when I looked in his eyes, I saw he wasn't at all. He was really sensitive. I had very clear images. He would begin on a downward spiral then, after about a year, he would come back from it and go on to be a superstar.

John made a note of my predictions, then he said, 'Take That made a statement that they are going to carry on as a band without Robbie. What do you think?'

The answer came clearly into my mind.

'No,' I said. 'They'll definitely split up within the year.'

John logged my predictions. His idea was to build up a dossier of my predictions and, when they came true, use them to enhance my credibility. He sent me pictures of Pamela Anderson and Tommy Lee. They were passionately in love and had just got married.

The minute I saw the photos, I saw Tommy Lee's rage. He had a slightly out-of-control look in his eyes. When I looked at Pamela, I could see she was trusting. I saw two children coming.

'It's a fiery relationship,' I told John. 'It will be on and off. It will finally collapse, but it will take a long time for them to separate.'

One morning, I was tidying the house with the television on. It was five days before the Queen's birthday and a presenter was talking about the preparations for the celebrations. Suddenly, I had an image in my head. I could see the Queen standing on steps with horses going past her (which I took to be the Trooping of the Colour). Then I saw a bomb blast inside a crowded building.

It was years since a vision had come into my head without me looking for it. I tried to get more information, but I couldn't get anything else. I told John, Alan and Mum, but without knowing where the bomb was going to explode, there was nothing I could do. I kept hoping I was wrong.

On the day of the Queen's birthday, I turned the television on. It was late morning and I was watching the horses troop past the Queen, when a newsflash appeared at the bottom of the screen. A bomb had just gone off in Manchester. Many people were hurt.

I was horrified. I felt so useless – so responsible. If only I had got the picture clearer, if I could only have recognized a landmark …

'Eric, what was the point in getting the information when I couldn't do anything about it?' I asked.

'You saw what would be,' he said. 'Not what might be.'

A few weeks later, I received a telephone call from a tabloid newspaper. John had shown the paper my celebrity predictions and they wanted to know if I would be interested in doing fortnightly predictions on Princess Diana now that she had split from Prince Charles. The plan was to get predictions from three psychics and then print them six months later, as a test to see who was the most accurate.

I was sent six large photographs of Diana, which I put on the wall in my middle room. It was strange; living with her photos, I got to know her very well. She was a funny mixture: she always needed approval, but the publicity was always meant for the best. She got a lot of stick but she was only trying to raise awareness of difficult issues.

Diana tended to see things and people in very black and white terms – they were either good or bad and she wanted to be good. She felt she needed to balance her life by giving as much as she received. She was trusting and easily manipulated. She never got a handle on being so famous. She needed to be loved, like all of us, but she didn't have a lot of people around her who loved her for herself.

The newspaper rang me a fortnight later. My first prediction was that she would make dramatic statements about her marriage in a TV interview. This was six weeks before the revelatory *Panorama* interview in which Diana said there had been three people in the marriage: her, Charles and Camilla Parker-Bowles.

Then I predicted she would get involved in international politics.

'Something to do with anti-war and children,' I said.

'She can't,' the paper's reporter told me. 'She's a member of the Royal Family and it's against protocol for her to get involved.'

A month later, Diana was photographed by the international press on the anti-land mine campaign. She was meeting children whose limbs had been blown off by land mines, exploding long after the war was over. She even walked through territory where unexploded land mines lay.

Then I saw a new man in her life.

'She's going to fall in love,' I said.

'What's he like?' the reporter asked. 'Can you tell us anything about him?'

'He has dark hair and tanned skin. He's either a sailor or he owns a boat. The only picture I have of them is by a white boat.'

Two weeks later, the news broke that Diana was seeing Dodi Al Fayed. The first picture to appear was of them on his white boat in the South of France. Then, from the boat, Diana baited the press, telling them she was going to make an announcement the following morning.

'What's it going to be?' the paper asked. 'What is she going to say? Are they getting married? Is she pregnant?'

I went to the photographs, but I couldn't see any announcement of any interest the following day.

'The other psychics we've asked have given us detailed descriptions,' the reporter said. 'You're not doing yourself any favours by saying nothing.'

'I'm sorry.' I was adamant. 'I don't see her saying anything. I'd rather not give a prediction than lie.'

The next day, Diana said nothing. It was a big wind-up.

The day before the newspaper was due to telephone again, I sat down with Diana's photographs to work on my predictions. All I could see were newspaper headlines with the words: 'They are gone.' I searched for images but I couldn't pick up anything.

'What do you think they're going to do this month?' the reporter asked me.

'I don't think I'm going to be much use,' I said. 'Some time this month, they seem to disappear off the face of the Earth.'

'What do you mean?'

'I can't find them,' I said. 'I don't know where they've

gone or why, but it will cause mayhem in the press.'

'Do you think they'll elope?' the reporter pressed for details.

'I don't think so,' I said honestly, 'but I really don't know what I am seeing.'

Two-and-a-half weeks later, Diana and Dodi were killed in the Paris underpass. I was up early that morning; I switched the TV on at about seven and that's when I heard that they were dead. My first thought was: 'That's why I couldn't find them.' I felt very sad for both their families. Living with Diana's photos for six months, I felt as if I had been involved in her life. Dodi, too – I always picked up that he was a kind and fun-loving man.

Watching television, I had a strong voice in my head.

'You've got to tell them about the ring.'

'What ring?' I asked.

'The ring Dodi bought Diana. His father knows about it.'

'Is it an engagement ring?'

'No, but it is a special ring.'

'How do I tell them?'

'Telephone the newspaper and tell them to ask Dodi's father. He is in his London home.'

I waited an hour before telephoning the paper. I knew they would be in chaos. But the voice would not leave me alone: 'Tell them about the ring.'

The reporter I usually spoke to was out of the office, so I delivered the information to a female journalist I didn't know.

'Dodi has had a ring made for Diana. His father knows where it is, but he's not going to talk about it unless he is asked. He should be at his London address.'

After I made the call, the voice stopped and I felt better. The next day, the front page of the newspaper carried a story and a photograph of the ring. I was not mentioned – and no one telephoned to thank me for the information. When I eventually rang the newspaper again, I was informed that the ring story had been filed by a freelance journalist. She had been paid £5,000 for it. She said she did not know anything about speaking to me.

In addition, the paper told me that the information I had been providing over the months was currently too sensitive to be used. All that work and accurate predictions and not a penny for it. I was behind on my rent and the electricity kept running out. Alan and I never had enough money to order coal; we sent the boys out to collect and chop wood.

When another national newspaper contacted me and asked if I had forseen Diana's death, I told them my predictions. If I could get proof, they said, they would print my predictions and pay me £15,000. When I told the reporter at the first paper, she went very quiet.

'Mia,' she said at last. 'I'm so sorry. We just shredded it all.'

'The Features Editor said he might run it at a future date,' I said. 'Why did you shred it?'

'We decided it wasn't going to be used so there was no point in keeping it.'

I knew she was lying. I asked her to make a statement confirming the predictions I made, but she said she couldn't help me make a story for another newspaper. It had all been for nothing. Tabloid journalism was clearly not the way I was going to get us out of our financial hole.

17

It was a cold, late October night.

'Come out into the garden, quickly,' Alan said. 'There are amazing lights in the sky.'

High in the sky were three massive transparent circular lights, through which I could see the clouds and stars. Their movements were smooth and circling, moving away from each other, spinning in formation, then resting in a triangle. It was as if they were involved in a choreographed dance.

Strange, amazing and heart-stoppingly beautiful. Neither of us was afraid, standing looking up, mesmerised.

'Where is it coming from?'

I looked across the fields. All was blackness – the nearest lights were tiny pinpoints from street lights a mile and a half away.

We had been standing there for about 20 minutes when the three lights suddenly rose high in the sky, then spun off in different directions very quickly. We were in a daze, discussing various theories – UFOs, spirits or car headlamps? I tried to ask Eric, but he would not reply.

Looking back, that was the beginning of a two-week countdown to tragedy. My greatest test was to come.

'Our relationship feels strange,' Alan said one night.

'What do you mean?' I asked. 'In what way?'

'We're more like brother and sister, aren't we?'

I thought about it.

'Yes,' I said. 'We are.'

We were both quiet.

'Do you think we should go back to being best mates?'

I said, 'I think that's what we've been all the time, Alan.'

'You all right, then?'

'Of course I'm all right.'

We smiled at each other and that was it. End of the relationship.

'Do you want me to move out?' Alan asked.

'Only when you want to,' I said. 'There's no rush, is there?'

Ending the romantic part of the relationship felt natural – Alan had voiced what, at some level, we both knew. It seemed no big deal to stop being lovers. It simply clarified what we were already living. Alan and I carried on sharing the same bed.

Alan did not have time to move out because, a few days later, I had a stroke. One minute I was making coffee, the next I was on the kitchen floor and two paramedics were putting an oxygen mask over my face.

I went unconscious again and came round in hospital. My body felt weird and it took me a while to work out why. The right side of my body felt different from the left; it was incredibly weak.

'We are going to give you an MRI scan to see what's going on,' the doctor informed me.

The scan showed that I had a large shadow on the left side of my brain.

'You've had a stroke,' the doctor said.

Two days later, I woke and my body felt normal again.

I told the nurse, 'I think I'm better.'

The doctor ordered another scan.

'The shadow has gone,' he said.

'It's fixed itself?'

'Impossible,' he said. 'A shadow of that size can't just disappear. It must have been a faulty scan.'

When I came out of hospital, Mum wanted to look after me at her house. I really needed to convalesce. But, when I rang home the first night to check that everyone was okay, I had a sense of panic. Something wasn't right.

When I got home the next morning, Shane was in the kitchen. He looked round and I saw bruises on his face. He had a black eye and his lip was puffed-up. While I was in hospital, Shane had been attacked on the platform at Queensborough railway station. But no one had told me because I was ill.

'Why?' I asked.

'I don't know, Mum,' Shane said. 'Even when I was on the floor, they kept kicking me.'

I felt terrible that I hadn't been there for Shane. Looking back, the shadow on my brain was a physical premonition of Shane's injury. But, at the time, Shane seemed okay. He went back to college the next day and I asked Steven, Luke and Paul to find other places to live. I really needed all my energy for Shane and Tanya.

Two weeks later, I got a call from Medway Hospital.

'We've got your son here,' a nurse informed me. 'Looks like he's had too much to drink and fallen over. He's knocked himself out. He'll come round soon. There's no need to worry.'

Alarm bells went off. Shane had never been paralytic drunk in his life – and he was on his way to the youth club where alcohol was banned. I could not get to the hospital fast enough.

'Shane.'

He was lying on a trolley in the Accident and Emergency Department. His eyes rolled.

'Help me,' he said. 'I fell off my hair.'

Shane wasn't making sense, but he certainly wasn't drunk.

'There's something wrong with Shane,' I told the doctor. 'It's not alcohol.'

'We see drunks like this all the time in A and E,' the doctor said. 'He's going to wake up with a bad headache.'

I thought of the scan I'd had two weeks earlier.

'He needs a scan,' I said.

But the doctor, convinced Shane was drunk, dismissed my instincts.

For 12 hours, there was no change. Shane made occasional noises, but he did not open his eyes.

'I can't believe you still think he's drunk,' I said to the doctor on his rounds. 'Why haven't you given him a scan?'

The doctor didn't look at Shane, he looked at Shane's charts.

'I think we should arrange a scan,' he said at last.

Another long wait. Shane began to roll around and bang his head against the metal bars on the side of his bed. I asked for blankets and wrapped them around the bars. He opened his eyes and I put myself in his line of vision.

'Shane.'

He did not recognize me. His eyes didn't flicker. I was desperate. I knew my son was in severe danger, but the hospital was not treating him as a medical emergency. There was no sense of urgency. We waited four hours for a porter to take him for a scan.

After the scan, the pace changed. Two nurses wheeled in an oxygen cylinder and a heart monitor. The porter took Shane back across the car park to the ward. It was a cold, windy day. I felt desolate. A gust of wind blew Shane's silver insulating blanket into the air. We were in a nightmare: my son was thrashing about on a trolley outside on the coldest night of autumn in nothing but his boxer shorts. The nurse leant on top of Shane to stop him falling off. I felt at the mercy of a system which wasn't taking proper care.

It was another two hours before Shane was transferred to the high-dependency unit at King's College Hospital, in London.

Just like when he was a baby, Shane's life was hanging by a thread. I kept thinking: Shane's been ill before, he always bounces back. He pulled through last time.

'You must be Mum.' The consultant breezed in with five doctors in tow. 'Shane has fractured the right side of his skull,' he said, 'and he has a large bleed on the left.'

At the time, I did not see the symmetry. The two shadows: one on my brain – now gone; the other on Shane's – threatening his life. In that moment, I was an ordinary mother and all I knew was that I felt powerless and scared. The gift of seeing is not an opt-out card. I had to ride the roller-coaster the same as everyone else, not knowing and not in control.

There was an operation that could have been done but the doctor wanted to wait. He was sure the shadow was temporary.

'He'll be fine in a few days,' he said.

But he was wrong. After he left, Shane made a bubbling noise in his throat. I shouted for the nurse and she hit the big red crash button above his bed. Shane was put on a respiratory machine and taken to intensive care. He was wheeled away, away from my protection.

Alan and I were taken to the waiting room in intensive care. Last chance saloon. Every minute that kept me away from Shane felt like an hour. Finally, we were allowed in to see him. The unit was like a space laboratory; high-tech machines were whirring and clicking and, at the end of each sloping bed, a nurse was positioned at a desk.

'Shane is on life support,' the consultant said. 'It sounds

alarming, but it often happens after a head injury. We'll give him a couple of days on life support to give his body a rest and then take him off. There is no need to operate.'

Shane's chest was rising and falling and I knew it was the machine that was making him do that. He looked so vulnerable.

Shane's nurse explained all the machinery.

'It looks daunting,' she said, 'but loads of people who've been on life support go on to make a full recovery.'

For two nights, we slept in chairs in the last chance waiting room. Then Shane was taken off the life support machine.

'What happens if he doesn't start breathing?' I asked.

But Shane breathed by himself. For three hours, Alan and I sat by his side, willing his every breath.

Shane said, 'I'm hot.'

It was the first normal thing he'd said since this nightmare began. His pyjama bottoms started to slip down and he yanked them back up.

'Oh God,' he said.

It was a total Shane manoeuvre and remark. He was coming back. He wasn't going to die.

'Shane is getting better,' the nurse said. 'Go home and rest.'

We went back to Kent, had a bath, some proper food, our own bed. In the morning, 16-year-old Tanya came back with me. Shane had been moved to the overflow bay of another ward. To my horror, I saw he had no monitor and there was no nurse in the room.

'Shane, Shane.'

His eyes, half opened, did not focus on me or show any recognition. I played my panic down to Tanya. Shane started moaning, just as he'd done before, banging his head against the bars at the side of the bed. Again, I asked for blankets to protect his head.

I was told, 'The doctor will come when he is available.'

Shane was making choking noises and brown liquid was coming out of his mouth and running down his face.

'We must get the doctor,' I said.

The nurse suctioned out Shane's mouth.

'This is very common,' is all she said.

Tanya looked terrified.

'Can't you do something Mum?' she kept asking.

Four hours later, the doctor arrived on the ward to do his rounds.

'The doctor is at the nurses' station,' a male nurse said.

I did not want to leave Shane.

'Please ask him to come in here,' I said.

'If you want to see him, you'll have to go to the nurses' station.'

Shane moaned and rocked. Tanya was by my side, holding onto me for support. How could I leave the room?

'Will you stay with Shane while I speak to the doctor?' I asked the nurse.

'Yes,' he said.

The doctor was standing at a desk, writing notes.

'Please come and look at my son. He's making strange

noises. His breathing is all wrong.'

'If your son is deteriorating the nurses will pick it up immediately.'

'Well they're not,' I said. 'Nobody's giving him regular checks.'

'I assure you,' the doctor said. 'If anything's wrong it will be picked up.'

'For God's sake, I'm only asking you to walk 20 bloody feet to look at my son.'

The doctor put his hand on my arm.

'I'm really sorry,' he said, 'but if I had to pacify all the parents in this hospital, I'd never get any work done.'

He turned to go.

'Condescending bastard,' I said.

I'd been left alone to fend for my son. I walked back to Shane's bed but, even before I could make out his shape under the blanket, I knew something was wrong. My chest clenched. There was no nurse in the room and Shane was not breathing. *He was not breathing.*

I shouted, 'Help, somebody please, help.'

The nurse ran in and hit the crash button. The doctor followed.

Shane looked lifeless, but he was resuscitated and put back on the breathing machine. I looked around for Tanya. A nurse found her curled up on the floor outside the unit and brought her back to me. She was shaking violently. I held her.

I told her, 'They've got him breathing again. It's all right.'

But it did not feel all right.

Shane was to have the operation he should have had three days ago. I arranged for my nephew Arron to come and take Tanya to Mum's house. I also rang Alan and asked him to join me. The operation took four hours. When it was over, the doctor came to see me.

'I'm afraid we couldn't save him.'

'He's dead?'

'Well, no,' the doctor said, 'not actually dead.'

'So he's alive?'

'Well, officially, yes, but it's really the machine.'

I did not understand.

'Is he dead or is he alive?'

'Officially he's alive. In nine or ten hours, we'll carry out a brainstem test to see if there's any activity in the brain.'

The doctor stood up.

'Please spend as much time with him as you wish. I'm really sorry.'

He walked out.

The pain was so intense – everything in me pushed to such a point of tension – I thought I must explode.

'It didn't have to happen.' The nurse at the end of Shane's bed was crying. 'He should have gone to the high-dependency unit. There's forms to make complaints,' she encouraged.

But all the fight had gone out of me. I stood by Shane's bed for 20 minutes, just staring at his face. He looked so young. My chest felt tight. I was dizzy. I needed some air.

Outside, on the steps of the hospital, I lit a cigarette. The night was crisp and cold and clear.

'Look at the sky,' Alan said.

This time there were five big lights – exactly the same as the ones we had seen over the cottage. They were making mad patterns in the sky. I thought: 'They've come to collect Shane.' 'Please go away,' – in my mind, I begged them. They were beautiful and magical, but I hated them.

I spent the rest of the night by Shane's bed.

'Please don't take him, please don't take him, please don't take him.'

All night it was my mantra. I had bargained with God – or whatever it was – when Shane was only one week old, tiny and helpless in an incubator. It had worked then. Shane had made a remarkable recovery – everyone said so. Why not now?

'Please don't take him, please don't take him.' I thought if I asked long enough and meant it strongly enough, Shane would live.

And as I asked, my fingers were softly tracing all over Shane's body – his fingertips, his palms, his wrists. I ran my fingers over his chest, down his legs – he was proud of his foot-baller legs – his feet – they were so soft – his lips, his nose, his ears, his neck.

I did it over and over again. I was imprinting Shane through my fingertips onto my mind.

And all the time, I soaked him in my tears.

The brainstem test showed that Shane's brain was dead. I was in shock. I could not believe Shane had been allowed to die.

He was just 18 years old. This was the first time I had asked for anything for myself, and Eric – God, spirit, the good energy I had been working with – had let me down. My prayers had not been answered. When I really needed help, they did not give it.

How would I tell Tanya – and Mum and Dad? I'd let them down as well as Shane. My arms felt empty. I wanted so much to hold him and make it better.

I went in to say goodbye to Shane. The machine was still making him breathe and he looked peaceful, asleep. I just wanted to be near him. I relaxed my body into the chair. I could do nothing but give in. All night I'd been fighting – I really thought that spirit would help me. But now all the fight had gone out of me.

A quiet voice in my head: 'Look for his aura, Mia.'

How extraordinary that I hadn't thought to look before. Then I saw with my own eyes: Shane's aura didn't exist any-more. His spirit was gone. It was as if someone had stolen him when I wasn't looking. In front of me was just a body with a machine making the chest go up and down.

Standing by Shane's bed, I looked through the small win-dow at the sky.

'So you took him,' I hissed. 'You took my son. You better look after him because one day I'm coming.'

Then I called Pete.

'Pete if you're around, please, please be with Shane. Don't leave him on his own because he's scared of the dark.'

Then I kissed Shane on his eyes, cheeks, nose – all over his face – and I said, 'Goodbye my son.'

It took three-and-a-half hours to get back to Mum's on the train. I had nothing to say, nothing to do. I just wanted to be on the move. Alan sat beside me, trying to say the right things. There were no right things.

Looking back, I realized that Shane had died when he had the respiratory arrest. While I was arguing with the doctor and he was refusing to look at Shane, Shane was dying. If I'd looked for his aura, then I would have known – and not spent the night willing him alive with my prayers. He left when the lights were in the sky.

The house was full of people – Arron, Jed, Angela, Mum and Dad. Tanya was screwed up in a tight ball on the couch. Tears were running like water down her face. I sat next to her and put my arms around her. Tanya cried herself to sleep and I lay beside her. She did not leave my side for two weeks.

I could not believe Shane was not going to be around any more. I found his football scarf. It still smelled of him. It was like being hit. I sat on the edge of his bed, holding his scarf. I wanted to hold him; I'd have settled for a cup of tea with him, or a moment's chat. I felt all my love for him, but the love hurt.

I made enquiries with the police and found out that Shane had been more badly beaten up than he'd let on at the time. He had been attacked by five lads who kicked him in the chest and head, even when he was on the ground. There were witnesses, but the lads were never found. Twice, in the week before he collapsed, Shane had such severe chest pains at college that they'd taken him to hospital. I was shielded from the truth because of my stroke – Shane didn't want me to worry. But my stroke was a manifestation of concern. I needed to worry.

Failure. I was a useless failure. I sat opposite Shane with his black eye and bruised lip and I didn't look any deeper. Why didn't I do a health scan on him? I should have known he would do anything to protect me from worry; I should not have believed him when he said he was all right. I should have known.

I was angry at myself and angry at Eric. For 14 years, I had felt I was Eric's pupil and he was my teacher. Our relationship was like the one between a father and daughter. And I had spent a lot of time helping him, doing the things that he wanted me to do. I had never asked him for anything for myself, for anything personal. This was the first time.

When I asked Eric to save Shane's life, I thought he would do it – or get someone else to. I couldn't believe that he let Shane die. It was the biggest betrayal. Did he know I was going to lose my son – and, if so, why didn't he warn me? He didn't warn me and he didn't help me. What sort of a father was that?

I was so angry. I wanted to retaliate. I wanted to do something bad – some terrible crime to hurt Eric. I was hurting like mad and I wanted him to hurt too. All those years of being on the side of 'good', doing the right thing, working – really working – at it. I shut down. Eric tried to talk to me but I refused to listen. My source of comfort had let me down and I would not be comforted by it.

I felt let down by the hospital too. The more I realized Shane was ill before he was admitted to hospital, the more I felt the system had failed in not taking his condition seriously. At the hospital I had been so isolated and ignored, I might as well have been alone with Shane on the top of a mountain. They didn't listen to me. In my opinion, they had not taken proper care.

I tried to get legal aid to help in my fight for answers, but I found that, because my son was 18 and single, the law said his death hurt less. If he'd been married, the legal system would have given him a monetary value. I had no hope of getting the case into court.

Two days before the Coroner's hearing, I went to see a local solicitor who was a friend of Pete's. I spent five hours with his legal books and turned up at the courthouse, more than prepared.

The police gave evidence and there were statements from the hospital. Shane's death was tragic – they all agreed – but there was nothing anybody could have done. At the end, the Coroner turned to me.

'I'd just like to ask you if there's anything you want to say before I give my verdict on the cause of death.'

'Yes, there is,' I said.

I stood up.

'I accuse King's College Hospital of manslaughter' – my voice was clear, every word distinct – 'through lack of care and through neglect.'

I consulted my notes and quoted a ruling law I had found

in the law book. It said that if a hospital grossly neglects or deliberately refuses to acknowledge or address a problem, then it can be answerable to manslaughter.

A big hush fell over the room. I'd said it. I sat down.

The Coroner looked at me.

'You do realize that's a serious allegation?'

'It's very serious that my son died,' I said. 'And he could have been saved.'

The Coroner shuffled his notes.

'I have no option but to adjourn this hearing,' he said, 'until a full representation can be given by all parties.'

At the next hearing, I sat opposite seven people representing the hospital; I was not allowed legal aid and I did not have the money to pay for a solicitor so I had no representation. There was no jury. The Coroner's verdict was 'Accidental Death'.

I wanted Shane to be buried near Pete. The Council said the plots were all filled, but a few hours later, someone rang – one was empty opposite Pete's; only a path separated them. Shane had collapsed 20 feet from the pub where Pete was stabbed. Two men I loved struck down in the same place. How could that be?

I chose Shane's favourite song for the funeral: Dire Straits' 'Brothers in Arms', blasting out at full volume. As his coffin was lowered in to the ground, I wanted to shout out, 'No – NO – Shane does not like the dark.' The afterlife felt meaningless. All I knew was that my child was going away from me forever.

I was in a panic. Mum was next to me.

'Mum.'

She looked at me. I could see tears running down her face. She had buried her grandson and her son.

'It's nothing,' I said.

I fought to regain control. He's not there, I told myself, he's gone, he's dead. You're only burying his body.

I couldn't watch the coffin go down. I did not look. All the time I was fighting to keep control.

Shane supported Liverpool and he'd never seen them play at home. He loved snooker and we always said we'd go to the Embassy World Snooker Championship. There were so many things we had planned to do and now we never would. I'd lost his future, seeing his life unfold – all those years to come. Shane was 18 years old; he had not even had the good bit yet.

I worried I would forget him – the way he looked, the sound of his voice. Then a memory would catch me unawares and it hurt. It was inconceivable to think I would not see my child again. This was not meant to happen. I had an enormous sense of shock. How could Shane's life end?

I felt guilty. Even with my special ability and the work I'd done, I couldn't save him. The whole thing was beyond belief. It hurt so bad – like someone was cutting into my flesh. There was a massive hole in the centre of my body. I felt I had lost 18 years of my life. All gone. Nothing left.

It was as if I had spent 18 years building a house; I had finally finished and was ready to put the roof on. But then, when I wasn't looking, someone swept it away. All those stones I laid with care, all the problems we overcame in building, all the sweat and hard work, all the energy and time. Suddenly it was not there. I had nothing to show for it. All that was left was barren earth.

Your kids don't die before you do. If only I'd done this, if only I'd done that. The self-recrimination was endless. Numbness and fury. I'd let my son down.

I thought of my stroke – my premonition ailment. What good did it do me? It took me away from my son when he needed me most. What was the use of my gift? It didn't help Shane. It was useless.

I asked a friend to cancel all my readings. I stopped answering the phone. There was no point to my work if it could not save Shane.

Tanya did not leave my side. Literally. She sat, lay, walked and ate alongside me. Her body pressed against mine. I could not cry, not in front of her. She needed me to be strong, so the tears stayed locked away.

I could control the emotional pain, but not the physical. There was a constant heavy pressure in my chest. I could not sleep; I could not eat. The thought of food made me nauseous. There was too much pain inside my body.

One afternoon, Arron came to take Tanya out for the first time and I waved goodbye to her on the doorstep.

'It's all right, love,' I told her. 'I will be here when you get back. You will be fine.'

She was white and pinched and fragile. I watched until she

was out of sight, then I went upstairs to my bedroom and closed the door. I remembered Shane as he was in the hospital, when I traced his body with my fingers. I brought that image back and I could see his face so clearly. I could feel my fingers going over the bridge of his nose, his cheekbones, across his jaw line and his brow.

As the picture came, so did the emotions. It was like a door opening on a tidal wave – it engulfed me. I sobbed for half an hour and then I had to stop. I pushed it all behind the door and closed it. Ten minutes later, Tanya came back.

Two weeks after the funeral, I walked down to the lake near the cottage. The mud was slimy beneath my trainers; the wind bit my face. I sat on a rock on the bank and looked at the grey expanse of water. Empty. There were ducks on the lake, but they looked two dimensional – as if they had no substance.

I came to the lake to be by myself – not because I liked my own company, but because it gave me a break from pretending that I was okay. I was barely getting through the days. It was such an effort to function, to try to be normal for Tanya. This place used to be special to me – I loved looking at the water and the birds. Now it was just somewhere to go. Its beauty meant nothing to me; it did not touch me. I could have been anywhere. The trees were black against the sky. Their bare branches looked brittle and lifeless, their sap drained away.

My mind felt clogged up, as if I was in a fog. I don't know how long I sat there; vacant, disappearing. It was an effort to be present. Back home, the drawers were stuffed with unpaid bills. There was a letter from the landlord threatening eviction. My world was falling apart but it did not matter: nothing was real.

'Mum.'

I did not expect Tanya to find me. She never came down to the lake, but, suddenly, there she was. I hadn't even heard her footsteps. I looked up. It was like waking from a dream. I felt I had never seen Tanya so clearly: her blonde hair falling around her face, her wistful look, a kind of fragility about her that tugged at my heart and made me want to protect her. This was the real world – my daughter in front of me, alive and hurting. Going away in my mind was a cop-out, an escape that I could not afford. I had to be there.

'Mum. A lady has turned up. You forgot to call her. She's come all the way from Essex.'

A reading? It was the last thing I wanted to do. I had no energy, nothing to give, no gift. I was about to ask Tanya to make excuses for me, when something stopped me. It was the look on her face, so weighted down and drawn. I could not ask her to do that for me.

'It's all right, love,' I said. 'I'll be there in a minute.'

As I walked back through the wet grass to the cottage, I realised I was freezing. I'd been sitting on a rock in my jeans and I had not noticed the damp seeping into my clothes and my bones. I felt weak. I had no intention of doing the reading and I decided to tell the woman I was not well.

She was in the kitchen, looking tired and pale. She was wearing baggy clothes and her hair was tied back in a band.

She hadn't bothered with make-up. She couldn't have been much older than 30. She looked as bad as I did. Her eyes met mine and I saw sadness. Something broke through my shell. I knew I could not turn her away.

I took her through to the little dining room. The curtains were still drawn from the night before and, as I opened them, there was sunlight for the first time that day. Usually, when people came for readings, I was ready and the room was tidy. Now I moved a pile of unopened post off the table and sat opposite the woman. How could I do a reading? Auto-pilot – it was the only way.

I had not opened up since the night I looked for Shane's aura and could not find it. My body relaxed as I calmed my mind. I felt more rested than I had in weeks. As I sat there in this peaceful state, I could make out a shimmering light. Right next to the woman stood a little girl, thin with a pale face and mousy-brown hair. She looked about nine years old.

My son had just died and I was seeing the spirit of a child. No spirit had ever had such an impact on me. She had come from where my son was now – the same place. I didn't try to speak, I was just looking at the little girl. I knew that she'd had a long illness, but hers was not a troubled soul. She spoke to me.

'This is my mummy.'

I looked at the woman.

'You've got a daughter in spirit.'

'Yes.'

'I had to go because my chest was really bad,' the child said. She looked so calm.

I repeated what the child said and the woman burst into tears. 'My daughter died of cystic fibrosis,' she said. 'Is she all right? Is she all right?'

'Thank you for giving me my teddy, Mummy.'

I saw a brown teddy bear with one eye.

The girl said, 'Tell her I'm okay, but I don't want her to cry anymore.'

Her last words before she disappeared were, 'I am all right.'

She was gone. I looked at the woman. Her eyes were streaming with tears, but she was smiling.

'Thank you so much,' she said. 'I put her teddy in the coffin with her.'

'Did it have one glass eye missing?'

She gasped, 'How did you know?'

At the door, she gave me a hug.

'You don't know how much you've helped me,' she said.

She did not know how much she had helped me.

I had been so caught up in my pain, enveloped by it and believing in it so completely, that it had obscured everything else. After the woman left, I had a sense of peace. That night, for the first time since Shane died, I opened up and called Eric. I saw him smiling at me, gently. I was pleased to see him again; it was a relief, like coming home.

'I've hated you for weeks,' I said. 'You and everyone else up there.'

'I know.'

'It hurts so bad, I thought it was going to kill me.'

'It won't kill you.'

Then he added, 'Nobody hates you or Shane. It's not personal. It wasn't against you. It was just time.'

When Shane was born, he was terribly ill and I prayed so hard for him not to die. Rather than having him stolen from me, perhaps I had been given an extra 18 years. As I talked to Eric, my attitude turned a hundred and eighty degrees. Instead of being angry, I felt deeply thankful for the time Shane and I spent together.

As Eric spoke, I realized I hadn't suddenly been abandoned by those I trusted. When things don't go the way you want them to, it doesn't mean fate – or God or spirit – is against you. It's not a big game plan for them to give you pain. The purpose of life is to realize our spiritual nature and things happen as they are meant to happen. Through Shane's death and its aftermath, I gained that understanding.

I'd gone to that rock-bottom place where I had no hope and come back with my faith strengthened. Shane's death took me to a deeper place inside. I had thought I was so special that Shane would be spared; his death taught me humility. It taught me that I'm an ordinary person – and that is magic in itself. There is so much to learn.

After talking to Eric, I could not sleep. I walked to the window and looked out at the night. There was a huge moon in the sky. How could I stop giving readings? I thought of the woman who'd lost her daughter. There is no spiritual balm for grief, but connecting with her child, knowing that her child was safe, returned hope to her. If I shared her pain then I could share her hope as well.

At that moment, I realized my gift was real. In the beginning, it was a game – almost an ego trip sometimes – now I was in awe of it. The capacity it had to heal, to connect us to those we love and the love we feel inside. I couldn't turn my back on my gift. Instead, I saw it like a path stretching out in front of me. It had a sense of complete rightness.

Clairvoyance means seeing with light. Like shining a torch in a dark corner, it illuminates what cannot be seen. Having my gift back did not take away the grief. I would never be able to touch Shane again – I would always miss his physical presence, the way he lumbered round the house and made silly jokes; his normal being, his Shane-ness.

But having my gift back did alter my relationship to the loss I felt inside. I no longer felt persecuted. I could experience the bigger picture, a sense of eternity. His spirit was safe and held somewhere. It was up to me now to let go. I would always miss Shane, but I did know that I would see him again.

Through the deepest pain, I gained the hardest lesson. Like all of us, I learnt through suffering. Now I can help others – and be helped in return. Clairvoyance can be a burden and a responsibility, but it also enlightens, showing us more of who we really are. I will always be thankful that I have been given the gift.

Make
www.thorsonselement.com
your online sanctuary